AF408319

Case Study: An Approach for Assessment of Water Pollution

Dhanushka Meegaswatte

CIP a Camerei Naţionale a Cărţii

Meegaswatte, Dhanushka.

Case Study: An Approach for Assessment of Water Pollution / Dhanushka Meegaswatte. – Chişinău : Generis Publishing (Online Marketing Group), 2020 (Print on demand). – 73 p. : fig., fot., tab.

Referinţe bibliogr.: p. 63-67.

ISBN 978-9975-4236-9-4.

504.45.054:556.53(282.253.27)

M 54

Cover image: www.pixabay.com

Generis Publishing
Online orders: www.generis-publishing.com
Orders by email: info@generis-publishing.com

TABLE OF CONTENTS

CHAPTER ONE: INTRODUCTION

1.1. Background to the Study

Comprising over 70% of the Earth"s surface, water is undoubtedly the most precious natural resource that exists on our planet. It sets the stage for the evolution of life on earth and is an essential ingredient of all life today (Marowski, 1992). There is no other resource that affects so many areas of the economy or of human and environmental health like water (Tavera, 2000). In view of this fact one would expect human beings to have the utmost respect for the resource and safe guard its cleanness. Yet throughout the world people are remarkably short sighted and negligent in this regard.

This study mainly base on Middle Canal (Meda Ela) of Kandy city, Sri Lanka which is known as an affluent of Mahaweli river. It has a complex catchment area with diverse type of land uses including densely populated urban areas. The Meda Ela has been modified by constructing concrete banks and paving the bed with cement at certain places. However, a major part of the canal still flows as a natural course. The banks of the Mada Ela have been reinforced by concrete walls from the point of its origin to about 100 m downstream. The canal flows underground (<1 km) from the sluice up to the Kandy railway station. The Meda Ela then merges out and connects with a network of waste water canals draining from various parts of the Kandy city. The banks of certain parts of the Meda Ela have also been modified by cement walls from the railway station up to the Mulgampola area (up to 3 km). Beyond Mulgampola, up to Getambe, the canal flows along a more or less natural course (Gajanayake et al.2015).

This Meda-Ela or middle canal which originates as an outflow of the Kandy lake, flows about 4 to 5Km along the southern boundary of the Kandy City collecting many by-streams mostly mixed with untreated wastewater releases on its before it finally confluence with the Mahaweli River at Gatambe. With rapid development and high population density, Meda Ela is increasingly getting polluted due to this direct disposal of solid waste and wastewater. Available literature highlights many untreated wastewater releases into the Meda-Ela from the central market, Hospital, Good-shed bus stand, Hotels and Houses etc.

The uppermost branch streams of the canal are being used by people for bathing, washing and even for drinking without purifying the water. Though the latter part of the canal is polluted, economic benefits are received by the people who are engaged in laundry business and the people who collect worms as fish feed. However, the majority pay additional cost for water purification due to results of direct dumping of waste into the canal (Abeygunawardane et al.2011.Urban water pollution has emerged as one of the most critical forms of environmental degradation in Asia. In Asian countries, water pollution is clearly an environmental and political issue. Water pollution, which is a common phenomenon in almost all Asian urban areas, results from the environmental impacts of urban growth, failure of regulations, and the increase of unplanned settlements with lack of basic sanitary and sewage systems. On the other hand, this is partly a result of the failure of the state institutions, weakness of central and local authorities and the historical negligence of environmental issues.

Previous studies that had been conducted on Meda-Ela had proved that the water quality of Meda Ela was not in a satisfactory level and it had been polluted due to many aforementioned reasons. Meda Ela is the main urban drain runs through Kandy city and it is one of the main storm water drainage canals which discharging storm water in the Kandy city basin into Mahaweli River. Since the canal is topographically situated at a low elevation, a large number of side canals drain into the Mid-canal with their heavy pollutant loads.Water from this affluent ultimately drains into the Mahaweli River.

Mahaweli is the largest river basin in Sri Lanka, draining about 16% (10,327 km2) of Sri Lanka's land surface. In recent times, with increasing population and rapid urbanization, settling around townships, especially on the banks of Mahaweli, has shown a marked increase causing significant pollution of this important water resource (Abeygunawardane et al,2011). On the other hand, Kandy, the second largest city in Sri Lanka, is believed to contribute a significant amount of pollutants into the headwaters through a number of tributaries including Meda Ela, Pinga Oya, Maha Oya, etc. around the city (Wijekoon and Herath, 2006).

Considering these facts we can assume that there might be a significant impact of Meda Ela on Mahaweli River. According to my knowledge the previous studies that had been focused on particular area (Meda Ela catchment) do not address the interconnection between Meda Ela and Mahaweli River. Therefore the main purpose of this study will be understanding the correlation between Meda Ela and Mahaweli River and determine whether Meda ela contributes a significant amount of pollutants into Mahaweli River that cause rapid increase of pollution level of the river.

Not only environmental perspective but also economical point of view in minimising or prevention of water pollution of Mahaweli River is beneficial to the society. For instance according to Abeygunawardane et al.2011 water treatment cost of the Greater Kandy Water Treatment Plant (which locates approximately 5km downstream to Meda ela confluence) can be minimized by enhancing the water quality of the River. The objectives which are addressed by this study help to comprehend the current status and identify appropriate water management strategies that could assist to minimize the water pollution in Meda Ela and eventually in Mahaweli River.

1.2. Research Problem

Meda-Ela is a natural water stream which starts from Kandy Lake, runs across the city and merges with the Mahaweli River. Over the years waste water generated by industries, garages, laundry community, hospital, bus stand and residences in the catchment of Meda-Ela has been released to the stream depleting its natural beauty and making it a waste channel. High rate of urbanization in the recent years has worsened the situation. The Middle Canal discharges its effluents into the Mahaweli at Getambe, upstream from the location of sacred water-cutting ceremony site and the location of the Kandy Municipal Council Water Intake. Therefore magnitude of pollution of the Mahweli River which occurs due to middle canal and its significance has to be identified.

1.3. Research Questions

How to assess the current water quality condition of Meda Ela - Kandy?

How does the pollution level of the Meda Ela and Mahaweli River fluctuate over the year?

Is there a significant impact of Meda Ela on Mahaweli River?

1.4. Research Objectives

To assess the current water quality condition of Meda Ela-Kandy;

To determine the pollution level fluctuation of Meda Ela and Mahaweli River over the year;

To confirm whether there is a significant impact on Mahaweli River from Meda Ela;

To propose management strategies for water pollution of Meda Ela and Mahaweli River;

1.5. Research Methodology

The first chapter covers the background of the study and it provides a justification for the research problem. Outline of the study is established through research questions and objectives. Literature review of this study mainly focuses on high quality articles / studies that are meaningful, important, valid and relevant, to the study area. It attempts to summarize, evaluate, and compare original research in the specific area. And also it provides a constructive analysis of the methodologies and approaches of other researchers. Once the issues identified and clarified in first two steps, it will be decided what data to collect, and how to collect it. Meanwhile it is considered which methodology to choose, and which methods to utilise within the methodology. The collected data needs to be analysed to provide answers to the research problem. Method of data analysis relates to the objectives of the research, that is the analysis will answer the research questions. Drawing conclusions relates back to the focused research problem. It will be evaluated how successful the research objectives were achieved and the strengths and weaknesses of the research will be highlighted.

1.6. Limitation / Delimitation

Water sampling will be carried out in Meda Ela as it covers upstream, downstream and the middle part of the canal. Sampling from Mahaweli River will be carried out in upstream and downstream of Meda Ela Confluence which is located 400m away from the Confluence. The physiochemical parameters which are measured will be limited to pH, BOD5, COD, DO, TDS.

CHAPTER TWO: REVIEW OF LITERATURE

This chapter aims to determine the current state of knowledge on water quality assessment and pollution management by discussing relevant water quality parameters and their significance in relation to river pollution assessment. It also reviews available literature on Meda Ela and Mahaweli River in order to build a strong basis for this study.

2.1 Introduction

The global water demand varies remarkably between countries; this depends on the population pressure, patterns of socio economic development, marked differences exist between developing and developed countries. Water supplies continue to decrease because of resource depletion and pollution, whilst population growth and expansion in industry and agriculture further exacerbate the problem of water scarcity. Contentious competition for the water of international rivers such as the Nile, the Jordan and the Ganges is a symptom of the increasing scarcity of water (Marowski, 1992). In the south Asian region distribution, occurrence and availability of water resources is uneven in the region and within individual countries, the water availability depends on the rainfall. There is a marked difference in water consumption at both global and regional levels. There is also an increasing trend of water scarcity leading to competition amongst different water users as well as amongst nations.

2.2 Water Pollution

The changes in impervious cover due to urban land use not only influence water quantity impacts, but also impact on the quality of receiving water bodies. Increased anthropogenic activities in urban areas increase pollutant generation and deposition on impervious surfaces. These pollutants are washed off during storm events resulting in high pollutant loads to receiving water bodies. As noted by Gunawardana. (2011), 50% of total river pollutants originate from storm water. These pollutants can alter the physical, chemical and biological processes in receiving water bodies. This alteration, in turn, can lead to adverse impacts on recreational activities and on the aesthetic quality of receiving waters (Settacharnwit et al. 2003).

The loads and types of pollutants incorporated into water bodies are dependent on the activities associated with the surrounding land use (Goonetilleke et al. 2005). Runoff from road surfaces, for example, has received considerable attention due to the abundance of harmful pollutants generated by traffic activities (Ellis et al. 1997; Herngren et al. 2006).

2.2.1 Pollutant Sources

Pollutants in the urban environment result from complex and diverse sources (Adachi and Tainosho 2005). The primary sources responsible for the accumulation of pollutants in urban surfaces are:

- Transportation activities
- Industrial, commercial and residential activities
- Construction and demolition activities
- Vegetation inputs
- Soil erosion
- Atmospheric fallout.
  (Brinkmann 1985; Pitt et al. 1995)

A Transportation activities

Transportation activities contribute large amounts of pollutant through vehicle traffic and road surface wear (Bannerman et al. 1993; Fulcher 1994). The rapid growth of transportation activities increases pollutant generation and the consequent pollutant load on road surfaces.

Transportation activities are the major source of sediments, metals and hydrocarbons in receiving waters (Walker et al. 1999; Wik and Dave 2009). Pollutants generated from vehicular traffic can be in solid, liquid or gaseous forms. These pollutants are mainly generated from:

- Combustion exhaust
- Lubricant leakages
- Abrasion products (tyre wear, brake lining)
- Load losses from vehicles
- Road surface wear
  (Brinkmann 1985; Bannerman et al. 1993; Adachi and Tainosho 2005).

The accumulation and generation of pollutants on road surfaces is very rapid. particles on road surfaces are subject to the complex mixing processes that occur during transport and other on-road activities. These processes continue to alter the composition of particles due to their interactions with the road through heat and friction (Beckwith et al. 1986).

These particles contain a wide range of toxic compounds that can leach to water and create toxicity in the environment (Evans 1997).

B Industrial, commercial and residential activities

Industrial, commercial and residential activities contribute a range of pollutants. Pollutant type and concentration varies with various land uses and their associated activities (Arnold and Gibbons 1996). Past researchers have noted that industrial sites generate relatively higher pollutant loads than commercial and residential land uses (for example, Sartor and Boyd 1972; Bannerman et al. 1993; Bian and Zhu 2008). Commercial activities can also introduce similar pollutants to urban runoff (Pitt et al. 2004).

In residential areas, activities such as lawn and garden maintenance and household cleaning contribute pollutants to urban surfaces (US EPA 2005). As noted by Bannerman et al. (1993), lawns and driveways contribute high phosphorous load in residential land uses due to the use of detergents. Fertilisers used in garden maintenance can contribute high nitrogen and phosphorus loadings to urban runoff. Furthermore, the addition of pesticides contributes to hydrocarbon loading.

C Construction and demolition activities

Construction and demolition activities contribute considerable amounts of pollutants such as solids particles, litter and chemicals are the most significant pollutants present at construction sites (US EPA 1993). However, the total amount of pollutants generated can vary considerably depending on the type of construction activity and the management of the site. Solids from construction sites are the major pollutant in storm water runoff. Brinkmann (1985) has noted that, in most cases during the wash-off, solids distribute according to their grain size. A high solids load can result in sedimentation in receiving waters (US EPA 1993).

D Vegetation inputs

Vegetation matter commonly found in urban areas includes plant materials such as leaves, grass, pollen and bark. These can clog pipes and drainage channels. Vegetation input can vary depending on catchment characteristics, land use pattern and seasonal variations. Vegetation matter is a significant source of nutrients and organic pollutants to urban storm water (Cordery 1977; Allison et al. 1998). According to the findings of Allison et al. (1998), nutrient contribution by leaf litter is relatively low compared to the total nutrient load.

E Soil erosion

Erosion is considered as a natural source of solids to runoff. Increased peak flow and high flow velocities, mainly contribute to erosion. Unpaved surfaces in urban areas, agricultural lands and construction and demolition sites are highly prone to erosion (Brinkmann 1985; Novotny et al. 1985). Loss of vegetation cover increases soil erosion. The severity of erosion varies depending on factors such as the soil type, land cover, climatic conditions, topography and intensity of rainfall (hydrological processes) (Farahmand et al. 2007). Furthermore, hydrologic change such as high peak flows has a significant influence on erosion.

F Atmospheric fallout

Atmospheric fallout originates as air pollution. Industries, vehicle exhausts and wind blowing over unprotected pavements introduces pollutants to the atmosphere (James et al. 1985). Vehicle exhausts emit dust particles to the air, and as the dust particles are small, they can remain in the atmosphere for a considerable time (Pitt et al. 2004). Therefore, emissions from these activities initially pollute the atmosphere and will eventually return to the ground surface as atmospheric fallout. Meteorological conditions such as rainfall, wind direction and wind velocity are influential parameters for dust fall (James et al. 1985).

2.3 Pollution and water quality from local perspective

Pollution of waterways is a serious environmental problem faced by the country today. Water is essential for all life forms and for industry.

Surface water bodies as well as groundwater aquifers become polluted due to the introduction of contaminating substances, such as domestic wastewater, industrial wastewater, and surface runoff contaminated with agrochemicals, solid waste, chemicals and oils/grease from domestic, industrial and commercial premises, leachate from solid waste landfills etc. (Ratnayake,2010).

The quality of water is affected by human activities and is declining due to the rise of urbanization, population growth, industrial production, climate change and other factors. The resulting water pollution is a serious threat to the well-being of both the

Earth and its population. Sri Lanka is acutely facing water pollution problem mostly due to increased human population sedimentation of water bodies is another adverse effect due to the improper agricultural activities in Sri Lanka (Senanayake *et al.* *2016*). Toxic chemicals then enter the county's water system and are delivered to other parts of the country, for example via the Mahaweli, Kelani, Walawe and Kalu, rivers causing health problems to those who rely on these water sources for their drinking water.

Domestic and industrial waste collected by municipalities and local councils is dumped either direct into the rivers or into garbage disposal sites close to the rivers. The accumulation of oxygen demanding wastes adversely affects aquatic life.

The algal blooms can be attributed to excessive amounts of raw sewage discharged directly into the water bodies. This provides organic matter, nitrates and phosphates which stimulate the growth of blue-green algae such as *Microcystis*. These nutrients enter the water bodies also due to industrial and agricultural activities. The addition of blue green algae increases the organic content of a reservoir thereby depleting it of vital oxygen required for aquatic life (Ileperuma,2000).

Large quantities of pesticides are increasingly used in Sri Lanka to sustain agriculture. Every year around 3000 tons of pesticides are sprayed over the environment and most of these finally end up in our waterways. Several pesticides with concentrations in the parts per billion (ppb) range were found in Mahaweli river water at Peradeniya (Ranatunga *et al.* 1996).

 Pollution due to excessive amounts of nitrogenous species such as ammonium, nitrite and nitrate is very common in areas of high population density and excessive fertiliser usage. In an earlier study, (Weerasooriya *et al.*1986) on the nitrate concentrations from shallow water wells in the Kandy district, it was found that the average nitrate content was around 2.5 ppm which is well below the WHO recommended value of 50 ppm. However, the validity of this standard as applied to a tropical country such as Sri Lanka is debatable since people consume far greater quantities of water than in a temperate country.

Pollution due to heavy metals can arise due to a number of reasons. Discharge of industrial effluents, deposition of motor car exhaust fumes and geological features of the soil are some of these factors (Ileperuma,2000).

However, two major sources of non-point source pollution are agricultural runoff and leachate from solid waste dumps, which are still not controlled by any legislation, nor are there any significant attempts at controlling these discharges (Ratnayake,2010).

2.3.1   Middle canal (*Meda Ela*)

Streams play a major role in an urban landscape. It serves water for domestic and industrial purposes. It maintains an ecosystem and adds aesthetic value to the city. However, in the recent past, those streams are used for dumping solid wastes and wastewater. The Middle-canal is an example for this unfortunate situation. The Middle-canal is considered the most polluted surface water body in the Kandy district of Sri Lanka. The catchment of Middle canal spreads in an area of approximately 13 Km^2. In recent times, with increasing population and rapid urbanization, settling around townships has shown a marked increase causing significant pollution of this important water resource (Abeygunawardane *et al.*2011). Since there is no proper wastewater disposal system, untreated domestic sewage is released directly into the Middle-canal (Abeysinghe, 2007).

In addition Middle-canal receives wastewaters from small scale industries such as commercial laundries, textile dyeing operations, various workshops, a hospital, and miscellaneous dischargers such as petroleum and other oily waste from motor vehicle workshops. Furthermore, since the canal is topographically situated at a low elevation, a large number of side canals drain into the Middle canal with their heavy pollutant loads.

 In addition, large water volumes from Kandy Lake spill over to the Mid-canal, especially during the rainy season. Therefore, polluted water in the Mid-canal is a potentially health hazard not only to the people living nearby, but also to persons the communities downstream (Jinadasa *et al.*2012).

2.4 Physical, chemical and biological water parameters

The health of a water body depends on the quality of its water, which is influenced by the presence of pollutants. The quality of water is generally assessed by a range of parameters, which express physical, chemical and biological composition of water (Meybeck and Helmer 1989).

2.4.1 Dissolved Oxygen

Dissolved oxygen (DO) is a measurement of the amount of oxygen gas dissolved in water, and available for use by plant and aquatic species (WHO, 2006). The oxygen content in natural water varies with temperature, salinity, turbulence, the photosynthetic activity of algae and plants, and the atmospheric pressure (Chapman, 1996). Oxygen gas naturally mixes with water through surface interaction; Fast moving waters typically have a higher DO due to mixing with air when the water hits debris such as rocks and logs. Oxygen concentration in natural running waters should be close to 100% saturation, that is, between 9mg/l and 11mg/l depending on temperature while concentration in unpolluted waters is usually close to but less than 10mg/l.

According to O'Neill *et al.* (1994) dissolved oxygen concentrations in drinking water produce no adverse physiological effect on humans; however, adequate amounts of dissolved oxygen must be available for fish and other aquatic animals. Different species and sizes of fish require different amounts of DO to thrive. Based on the U.S. EPA"s water quality criteria, the one-day minimum for cold-water species is 5mg/l in early development stages and 4mg/l for other stages. For warm water species, 5.0 mg/l and 3mg/l is needed in early and other stages, respectively (Aull, 2005).

Oxygen concentration in unpolluted water is close to but less than 10 mg/l, while in running natural waters DO should be close to 100% saturation (between 9-11 mg/l). DO have no health impacts on humans but an aquatic organism requires certain DO concentrations.

2.4.2 Water pH

pH is a measurement of the acidity or alkalinity (base) of a solution. When substances dissolve in water they produce charged molecules called ions. Acidic water contains extra hydrogen ions (H+) and basic water contains extra hydroxyl (OH-) ions (Mesner and Geiger, 2010). Water pH is closely linked to biological and chemical processes within a water body and all processes associated with water supply and treatment (Chapman, 1996). The pH is measured on a scale from 1.0–14.0 with no units, where more basic solutions have a higher pH and more acidic solutions have a lower pH, the pH of 7.0 being neutral. Each whole unit on the scale represents a multiplication factor of 10. Thus, water with a pH of 5.0 is 100 times more acidic than water with a pH of 7.0 (Mesner and Geiger, 2010). Water pH is generally not a problem itself, but it is an indicator of other problems such as Sodium and Carbonates. A decrease in pH increases the corrosivity of water, and increasing the pH increases the tendency to precipitate mineral scales such as calcium carbonate.

According to Aull *et al* (2005) several factors can be affected by the pH of water, including biological availability and solubility of elements in water. Growth and reproduction of freshwater aquatic species of fish are found to be ideal within a pH range of 6.5 to 8.5; although they may thrive slightly outside this range, pH below 4 or above 10 will kill most aquatic animals (Mesner and Geiger, 2010).

It seems that Water pH is not a problem by its self but it is closely linked to all biological and chemical processes within a water body.

2.4.3 Biochemical oxygen demand

The biochemical oxygen demand (BOD) is used to read the level of biochemically degradable organic matter or carbon loading in the water. It is usually defined by the amount of O_2 consumed by the aerobic micro-organisms present in the water sample for the purpose of oxidising the organic matter and to convert it to a stable inorganic form (Chapman and Kimstach 1996; Liston and Maher 1997). Hence, in water quality analysis this parameter is used to determine the biodegradable organic content of the waste in terms of O_2 which is required when the wastes are discharged into natural water where aerobic condition prevails.

As the wastes which contain biodegradable matter are released into a body of water, microorganisms, especially bacteria, feed on the wastes and break them down into simple organic and inorganic substances. During this decomposition in an aerobic environment, the process produces stable end products such as carbon dioxide (CO_2), sulphate (SO_4), orthophosphate (PO_4) and nitrate (NO_3). The process can be represented by the following form (Masters 2004, p.117):

$$\text{Organic matter} + O_2 \xrightarrow{\text{Micro-organisms}} CO_2 + H_2O + \text{New cells} + \text{Stable products}$$

The BOD is usually determined through standardised laboratory procedures where the sample is incubated in the dark at a steady temperature of 20 ^{0}C for the duration of 5 days, thereby measuring the amount of O_2 consumed in this process. This explains the term BOD_5 (biochemical oxygen demand on five days). Unpolluted waters typically contain BOD_5 values of 2 mg/L or less, while raw sewage could have a BOD_5 value of about 600 mg/L (Chapman and Kimstach 1992). BOD_5 values are often used as a robust surrogate of the degree of organic pollution in water body as it can accurately depict real world impact on receiving waters.

2.4.4 Chemical oxygen demand

The chemical oxygen demand (COD) is used to indirectly measure the amount of organic compounds in water. Most applications of COD determine the amount organic pollutants found in surface water, making COD a useful measure of water quality (Harrafi et al, 2012). It measures the O_2 equivalent of the organic matter present in a water sample that can be oxidised by a strong chemical oxidant, such as dichromate or permanganate (Chapman and Kimstach 1992). It is expressed in mg/l, which indicates the mass of oxygen consumed per litre of solution. The 2 to 4 hour laboratory tests for COD measures the level of O_2, which is necessary for chemical oxidation of organic and inorganic matter in the water sample to convert into CO_2 and water. The COD test does not aim to identify the oxidisable material or find differences between the organic and inorganic material in the water. However, it has been a widely used measure for water quality analysis over the past several decades. The concentration of COD observed in unpolluted surface water remain around 20 mg/L or less, while values are normally greater than 200 mg/L in effluents (Chapman and Kimstach 1992). It is noted that COD measurements are usually higher than the BOD_5 measurements (Masters 2004).

2.4.5 Total Dissolved Solids

The salts or total dissolved solids (TDS) in water determine the salinity (Grattan 2002). Salinity is stated as TDS in mg/l. It is often determined by measuring the electrical conductivity (EC). EC is determined by the amount of dissolved solids in water. EC is related to salt content; i.e. the higher the salt content, the higher the EC will be (Anhwange et al., 2012). An increase in conductivity of the water indicates the addition of mineral salts to the water (Gupta et al., 2009). TDS value in mg/L is about half of the electrical conductivity (μS/cm) (Stone et al., 2013). TDS is formed due the ability of water to dissolve salts and minerals and these minerals produce un-wanted taste in water (Mohsin et al., 2013).

2.5 Similar Case studies

Abegunawardana *et al* (2009) assessed the status of water quality in Meda Ela and to link the pollution levels with the status of the surrounding physical and human environment. They also attempted to assess the impact of water pollution on the society. Water quality of Meda Ela was monitored for physical, chemical and biological parameters at monthly intervals for six month period during May-October.

Table 2.1: Measured Chemical and Biological Parameters in Meda Ela

Chemical Parameters	Biological Parameters
TDS (mg/l)	Total coliform (1/100ml)
Conductivity (µs/cm)	E.coli (1/100ml)
Ammonium (mg/l)	Presence of aquatic fauna spp.
Nitrite (mg/l)	
Nitrate (mg/l)	
COD (mg/l)	
BOD5 (mg/l)	
DO (mg/l)	

Source: Abegunawardane *et al.*, 2009

Water samples had been collected at monthly intervals from seven sites. Out of them, three sample sites had been located in a branch of the main canal and the rest were located along the main canal at upper middle and lower sections and at the confluence of Mahaweli River.

Table 2.2: Location of sampling in Meda Ela

ID	Description	Location
L1	Abundant Hilly area	
L2	Residential area with commercial establishments	Branch Stream
L3	Residential area with Commercial establishments	
L4	Highly commercial area/Kandy town	Starting point of Meda-Ela near to Kandy lake outlet
L5	Residential area with Commercial establishments	
L6	Residential area with Commercial establishments	Middle and latter pan of Meda-Ela
L7	Residential area with Commercial establishments	

Source: Abegunawardane *et al.*, 2009

As per the results, from the upstream to downstream total dissolved Solids (TDS) and conductivity showed an increasing trend. The highest TDS (241 mg/l) was reported in June at L5.

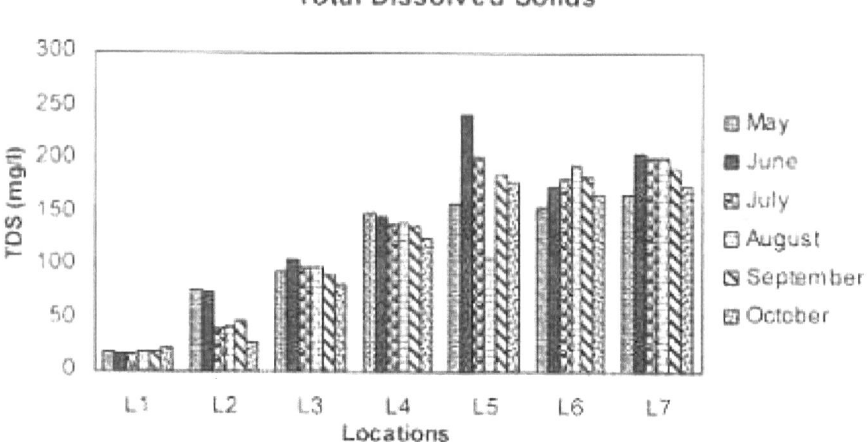

Figure .2.1. Spatial Variability of TDS in Meda-Ela

Source: Abegunawardane *et al.*, 2009

The conductivity values of Meda Ela had reached up to 458µs/cm indicating the presence of high concentration of dissolve ionic salt. In line with TDS, conductivity was also noted to be gradually increasing towards downstream. The reported Dissolved Oxygen (DO) values were below the standard of 5 mg/l for fresh water which is an indicator of poor water quality. DO values of less than 5 mg/l was a good indicator of high organic matter content in the water, all the values of COD were under the tolerance limit of 250 mg/l.

The values below 30 mg/l of BOD_5 are accepted for wastewater that is discharged in to surface waters. In this case water in Meda Ela was within this tolerance limit. However BOD did not show a pattern of variation along the canal though it was noted high at some sampling locations. Furthermore high concentration of nitrogen species (Nitrate, Nitrite, and Ammonium) was reported from the last three sampling locations due to drainage of all the wastewater of Kandy city from various parts of the hilly terrain. However, the water samples had not showed extremely high nitrate levels. Eventually this study revealed that Meda Ela water was polluted at different levels from upstream to downstream.

Jinadasa *et al* (2012) attempted to examine the water quality status of the *Meda Ela* and possible impacts of the nearby residents on water quality. They had carried out a water quality assessment at 11 locations along the Mid-canal to analyse physical, chemical and biological parameters for both the wet and dry seasons. Sampling was conducted at approximately equal distances along the length of the canal.

Table 2.3: Location of sampling and the distance from Mid-canal starting point

	Location—Along Mid-canal	Point sources	Distance from the Mid-canal starting point (km)
1	Outlet of the Kandy Lake		0.00
2	Atupattiya (The point it reappears through a tunnel close to Mallika Studio)		0.50
3	Goods shed (The point it goes underground close to Goods shed Bus stand)		0.80
4*	Hospital treatment Plant effluent—I	√	1.90
5*	Wastewater from cloth washing tanks	√	1.95
6	Upstream to Suduhumpola Junction		2.00
7*	Slaughter house effluent	√	2.20
8	Downstream to Heeressagala Junction		3.25
9*	Effluent of court complex	√	4.30
10*	Hospital treatment plant effluent—II	√	5.25
11	End of Mid-canal		5.30

Source: Jinadasa *et al,*2012.

Results of the water quality assessment showed increase in the water quality deterioration towards the end of the Mid-canal.

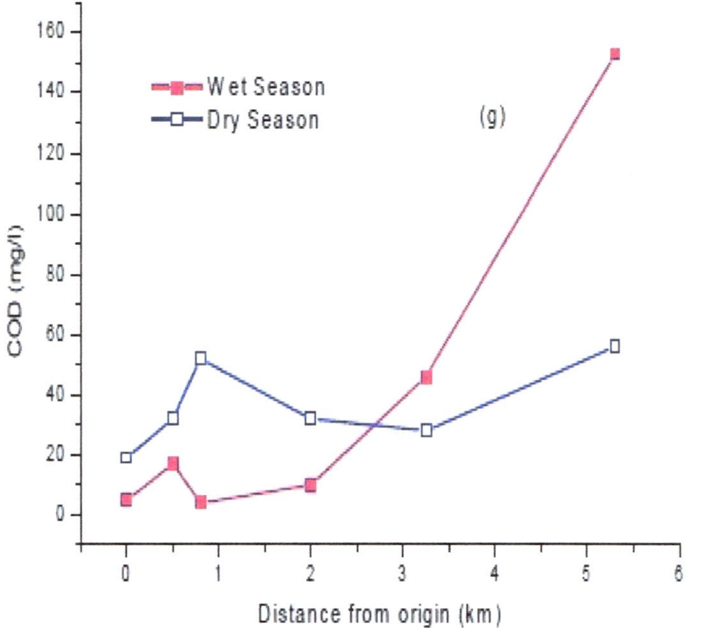

Wet Season
Dry Season
(g)
COD (mg/l)
160
140
120
100
80
60
40
20
0
Distance from origin (km)
0
1
2
3
4
5
6

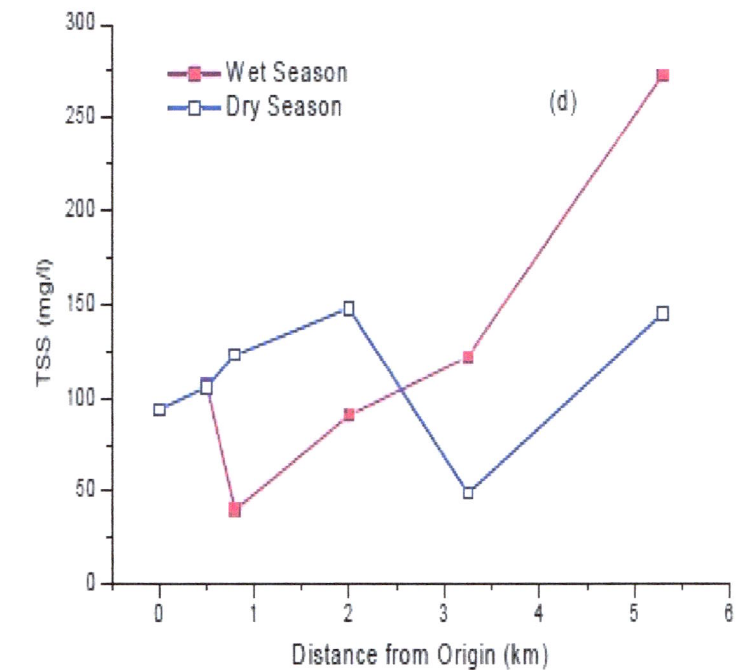

Wet Season
Dry Season
(d)
TSS (mg/l)
300
250
200
150
100
50
0
Distance from Origin (km)
0
1
2
3
4
5
6

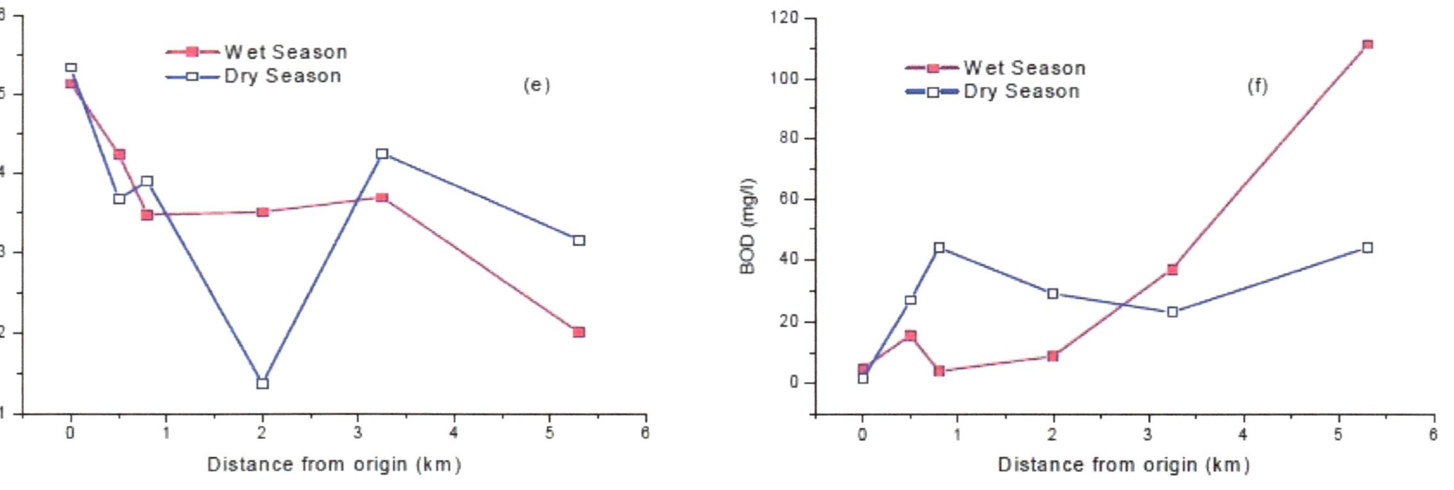

Figure 2.2. Water quality variations along the Mid-canal

Source: Jinadasa *et al*,2012.

The water quality analysis along Mid-canal indicated the pollution level in the wet season was high. Dissolved oxygen was low at the end of the canal and especially so in wet season. Total suspended solids values had exceeded the discharge limits at all locations along the canal. The concentration of BOD5 and COD increased towards the end of the Mid-canal.

Perera *et al* (2013) investigated the DO concentration variation along the Meda-Ela to determine the critical and regaining areas. They collected water samples at nine points along the stream starting from the Kandy Lake to the outlet of the canal where it confluence with the Mahaweli River. DO concentration had been measured for each water sample in the same month in 3 years, 2010, 2012 and 2013.

Table 2.4: Location of sampling and the distance from Kandy Lake

Locations	Sampling Point	Distance from Kandy lake (km)
Kandy Lake	A	0
Beginning of the Spill	B	0.09
End of the Spill	C	0.11
Near "Deiyanwala" ground	D	1.60
Near the Fire brigade	E	2.00
Near Royal Mall Complex	F	4.35
Near Court complex	G	4.68
New Lawyers complex	H	4.92
At the Outlet of the canal.	I	5.62

Source: Perera *et al* ,2013.

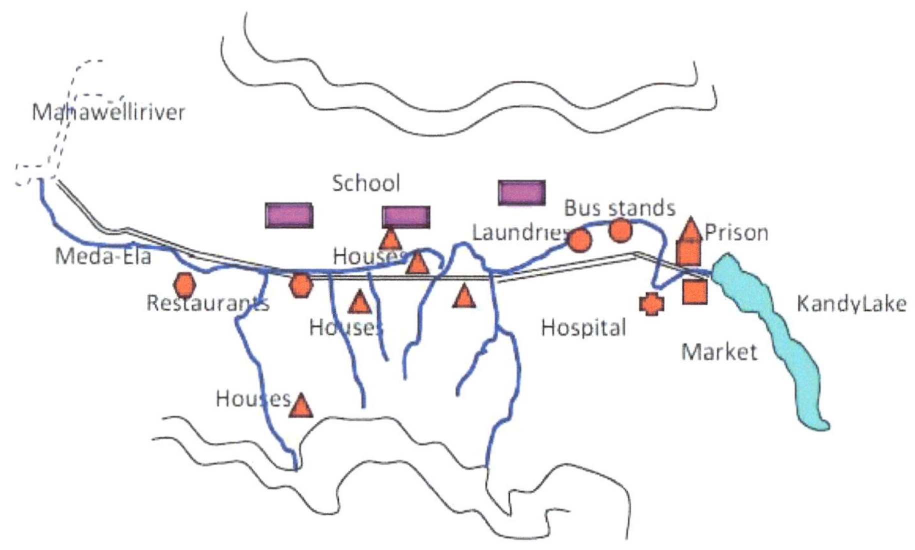

Figure 2.3: Geographical illustration of the Meda-Ela and surroundings

Source: Perera *et al* ,2013.

Their results in Meda-Ela show how a natural stream lost its characters due to urban and domestic activities in the catchment area. The reduction in DO concentration increases over the years. At some sampling points the DO concentration had reduced at an alarming rate. They had identified as critical area of pollution in the Meda-Ela from Lake Spill to Fire brigade, where the DO has decreased from 5.8 ppm to 0.8 ppm . These areas are the most sensitive due to high urban activities that include the Good shed bus stand, hospital, prison and the market.

Dhaka is second polluted mega cities in the world. It is bounded by rivers, inter-connected with canals which have always formed a support for the city residents. Though Industries are minor users of water in terms of quantity, but have significant impacts on surface water quality. Effluent of this industrial area is directly discharged into Begunbari and Narai canal which carries the waste through Balu River and ultimately flows on Sitalakha River which is used in Saydabad water treatment plant for meeting water consumption demand of Dhaka city dwellers. In order to evaluate the current situation Roy *et al* (2014) investigated the water quality of Balu River and Narai cannel.

The study area was located at the Tajgaon metropolitan area in Dhaka district. The location was selected as the industrial effluents discharged directly from Tejgaon industrial area into Begunbari and Narai canal which ultimately flows on Sitalakha river via Balu river.

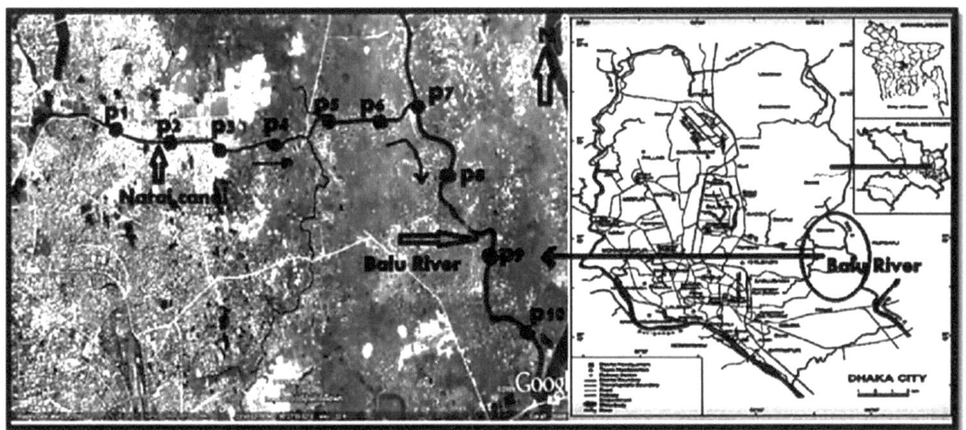

Figure 2.4: Study area and sample points

Source: Roy *et al* ,2014.

They had collected the water samples from different points of the Narai canal and Balu River during January to June 2012. From the Narai canal, 3 samples had been collected from each of upstream and downstream. From Balu river, 2 samples were collected from each of upstream and downstream. They had measured water quality parameters including pH, Total Dissolved Solid, Dissolved Oxygen and NH_4.

Table 2.5.Water quality parameters at sampling sites of Narai canal and Balu river

| Water quality parameters | Narai canal (Sampling points) | | | | | | Balu river (Sampling points) | | | | Range |
| | Narai canal (u/s) | | | Narai Canal (d/s) | | | Balu river (u/s) | | Balu river (d/s) | | (Narai canal |
	P1	P2	P3	P4	P5	P6	P7	P8	P9	P10	to Balu river)
TDS (mg/L)	1308	1288	1105	1106	1103	1101	1015	1010	1006	982	982-1308
pH	7.03	6.89	7.08	7.22	7.25	7.33	7.33	7.33	7.31	7.28	6.89-7.33
NH_4 (mg/L)	89.76	64.48	49.38	42.57	47.63	36.31	27.58	22.47	14.45	6.79	6.79-89.76
DO (mg/L)	0.45	0.37	0.33	0.38	0.35	0.34	0.37	1.21	1.66	2.12	0.33-2.12

Source: Roy *et al,* 2014

As per the results, TDS value had increased dramatically specially in Narai canal. The DO values were recorded ranging from 0.33 to 2.12 ppm at different points. The lowest mean value (0.36 ppm) was observed in Narai canal downstream. Analysed data suggested that the Balu River was heavily polluted with organic and human wastes, as indicated by the low DO. The ammonium (NH4) at different sampling points ranged from 6.79 - 89.76 mg/L and most of the points had shown above or near 30 mg/L. It is also observed from this study that within 7 years (2005-2012) this ammonium value had increased dramatically specially in Narai canal which is highly hazardous for agriculture and a sustainable environment.

The results of this study had revealed that both the Narai canal and Balu river water were neutral with suitable pH value. On the other hand, in most of the points the values of other three parameters, i.e. TDS, DO and NH4 were found to be highly vulnerable condition. This water is not only detrimental for human health and aquaculture but also unsuitable for irrigation practices.

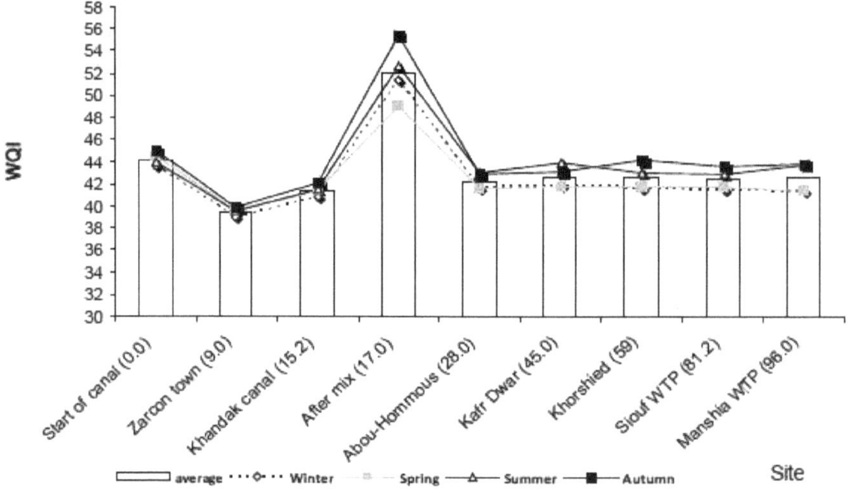

Figure 2.2 Water Quality Index of Mahmoudia canal

Source: Abdullah AM, Hussona ED, 2014

The main water source for Alexandria and Behiera governorate which locate at northern west of Egypt is Mahmoudia canal. The canal receives domestic and agriculture wastes from Zarcon Drain and other non-point sources. Abdullah and Hussona (2014) offered comprehensive water

quality information of Mahmoudia canal. They collected one hundred and twenty water samples from ten stations. Ten samples were collected monthly, starting from June 2011 to May 2012 and they measured Temperature, pH, Dissolved Oxygen, Electrical Conductivity, Heavy metals, Chemical oxygen demand, Biological oxygen demand, total organic carbon, Total hardness, pesticides, Total algal count, Total plate count, total coliform and faecal coliform in each sample. Results showed the seasonal and spatial variations of Mahmoudia canal parameters (physical, chemical and biological) from June 2011 to May 2012. To verify data of the most influential factor among the stations of Mahmoudia canals; they performed cluster analysis using Word's method (linkage between groups), with Euclidian distance as a similarity measure.

Finally they found out that main water quality was exhibit high pollution levels that create health risks at present, indicates unsafe levels of pollution for direct use in drinking water, irrigation and fisheries. Furthermore the major sources of pollution in Mahmoudia canal are discharge of Zarcon drain.

Al-Mashagbah (2015) evaluated the water quality of King Abdullah Canal and Jordan River using the water quality index method (WQI). For this purpose, nine different sampling sites were used in the calculation of WQI during the period of January to December 2012. The samples were analyzed for various physico-chemical parameters such as pH, electrical conductivity, total suspended solids, and ions of Sodium, Potassium, Calcium, Magnesium, Fluorite, Chloride, Sulfate, Bicarbonate, and Nitrate in different seasons.

Table 2.6 Arrangements of sampling sites

S. No	Sample code	Site name
1	JV1	King Abdullah Canal
2	JV4	King Abdullah Canal
3	JV6	King Abdullah Canal
4	JV7	King Abdullah Canal
5	C2	King Abdullah Canal
6	CX	King Abdullah Canal
7	JR1	Jordan River
8	JR2	Jordan River
9	JR3	Jordan River

Source: Al-Mashagbah, A.F. 2015

The analysed results have been used to suggest models for predicting water quality. The computed WQI for the nine samples has a range from 46.66 to 542.08. The analysis reveals that the water quality status of the study area is varying from excellent to good in the upper part of the canal and from poor to very poor in the lower part of the canal.

Table 2.7 Water Quality Index Values of the Canal and the River

Site No.	Site code	Sampling point	WQI	Water quality
1	JV1	King Abdullah Canal	60.48	Good water
2	JV4	King Abdullah Canal	46.66	Excellent water
3	JV6	King Abdullah Canal	53.12	Good water
4	JV7	King Abdullah Canal	56.48	Good water
5	C2	King Abdullah Canal	104.28	Poor water
6	CX	King Abdullah Canal	101.83	Poor water
7	JR1	Jordan River	542.08	unsuitable for drinking
8	JR2	Jordan River	226.14	Very poor water
9	JR3	Jordan River	522.19	unsuitable for drinking

Source: Al-Mashagbah, A.F. 2015

The results indicated that the lower part of the canal is polluted. Therefore, the water is not safe for domestic use and needs further treatment, especially in the lower part of the canal.

CHAPTER THREE: METHODOLOGY

3.1 Background

Temporal and/ or spatial water quality changes in an area can be influenced by many factors; waste releases from various activities, variable rainfall, variable runoff, Variable River flows, natural disaster etc. In addition it is important to understand and recognize that a water quality parameter very critical to one location may not be so critical to another. Therefore it should be very selective in choosing the sampling locations and monitoring parameters.

3.2 Research Methodology

3.2.1 Identification of dry season and wet season

In the analysis part, this study only focuses on primary data which would be collected in dry season and wet season of 2018. However conclusions of previous studies will be incorporated with the discussion of this dissertation as secondary data.

Prior to commence water quality monitoring these two different seasons of the year had to be verified. As a preliminary step, historical rainfall data were studied in order to identify the dry season and wet season of the year. Following figure shows average monthly temperature and rainfall in Sri Lanka from 1901 to 2016. Basically rainfall in Sri Lanka has multiple origins. Monsoonal, Convectional and Depressional rain accounts a major share of the annual rainfall.

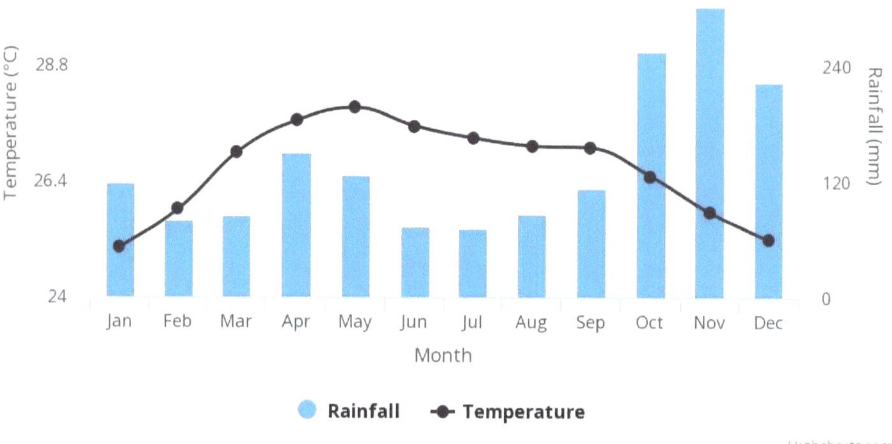

Figure 3.1: Average monthly temperature and rainfall in Sri Lanka from 1901 to 2016

Source: World Bank -Climate Change Knowledge Portal (CCKP)

In accordance with the above graph, we can observe that Sri Lanka receives comparatively low rainfall in first and third quarter of the year than second and fourth quarter. However this research attempts to ascertain the surface water quality parameters in Kandy area. Therefore rainfall in Kandy area has to be considered as well. Kandy does experience a drier period from January to April. From May through to July and October to December the region experiences its monsoon season, during this time the weather is rough and unstable. From March through the middle of May is the inter-monsoonal period. In order to confirm this statement, rainfall data of past few years in Kandy area were studied. Following figures demonstrate the monthly variation of rainfall in Kandy from 2014 to 2017.

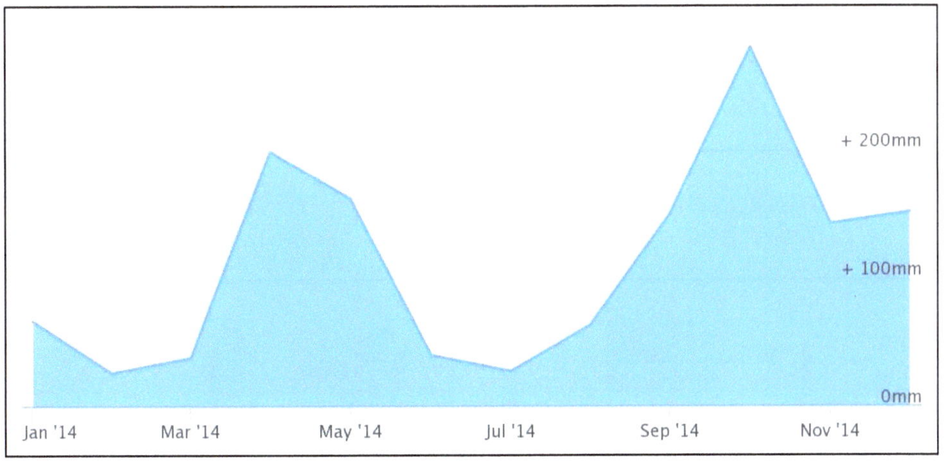

Figure 3.2: Average monthly rainfall in Kandy -2014

Source: worldweatheronline.com

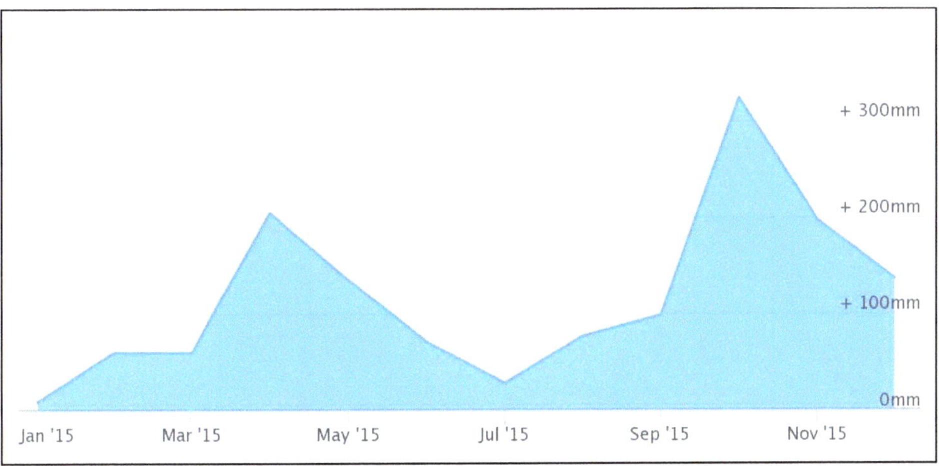

Figure 3.3: Average monthly rainfall in Kandy -2015

Source: worldweatheronline.com

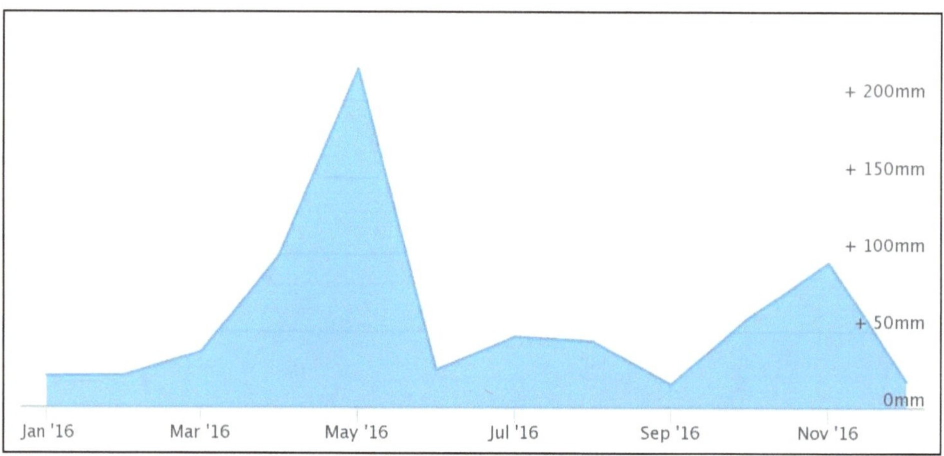

Figure 3.4: Average monthly rainfall in Kandy -2016

Source: worldweatheronline.com

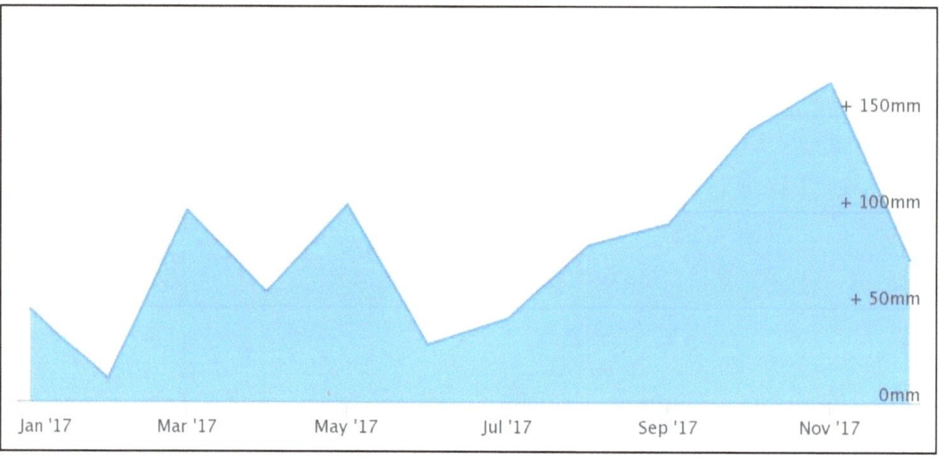

Figure 3.5: Average monthly rainfall in Kandy -2017

Source: worldweatheronline.com

Considering above information and facts we can conclude that the driest season of Kandy is first quarter of the year and the wettest season of the year is fourth quarter. Once we compare rainfall data of past few years, we can identify that February is the month that receives lowest precipitation of the year. Generally Kandy receives comparatively high rainfall in October as a result of second inter-monsoon. Consequently it was decided to conduct the water quality monitoring in February and October respectively for the dry season and wet season.

3.2.2 Sampling site selection

Prior to performing the water quality monitoring, number of site reconnaissance visits was made to identify the most suitable locations for sample collection that address the objectives of the study. The sampling sites were chosen to reflect on different activities along the Meda Ela and Mahaweli River that could be affected by the change in water quality. The main criteria considered in study site selection were determined by the anticipated variation in physical and chemical properties of water.

One of the main objectives of the study is to determine the pollution status fluctuation of Meda Ela and Mahaweli River. Therefore sampling locations shall represent both Meda Ela and Mahaweli River. The catchment area of Meda Ela is comparatively complicated than the catchment area of particular section of Mahaweli River. For instance Meda Ela flows thru highly urbanized and congested environment. And also within the route of the canal, there are some establishments / facilities that might provide significant contribution for water pollution. As a result of this environmental condition, it was identified 2 sampling locations in Kandy Lake which is the origin of Meda Ela and 3 locations in Meda Ela . These 5 locations were selected in approximate similar distances as represent the entire canal and the unique characteristics of each location were also considered prior to select particular location.

In order to confirm whether there is a significant impact on Mahaweli River due to Meda Ela obviously we should identify the water quality variation of Mahaweli River once Meda Ela discharges in to the River. Consequently, 2 locations were selected in Mahaweli River that locates upstream and downstream to the Meda Ela confluence.

Table 3.1: Description of sampling locations

Location ID	Location	Description
ME1	Inflow from Ampitiya	One of the main inlets of Kandy lake and it is the furthest point from Lake Outlet. (N $7^0$17' 18.02, E $80^0$38' 47.33)
ME2	Kandy Lake Outflow	The point where Meda Ela originates (N $7^0$17' 28.82, E $80^0$37' 13.94)
ME3	Deiyannewela Bridge	End of Underground Section (N $7^0$17' 10.83, E $80^0$38' 44.31)
ME4	Heeressagala Junction	Heavily congested area at Downstream of Meda Ela (N $7^0$17' 38.25, E $80^0$38' 1.22)
ME5	Meda Ela Confluence	Discharge point of Mede Ela

		(N $7^0$17' 17.10, E $80^0$38' 17.64)
MR1	Upstream of Mahaweli River	400 m upstream to Meda Ela Confluence (N $7^0$17' 8.61, E $80^0$38' 8.31)
MR2	Downstream of Mahaweli River	400 m downstream to Meda Ela Confluence (N $7^0$17' 28.74, E $80^0$38' 22.26)

Source: Prepared by Author

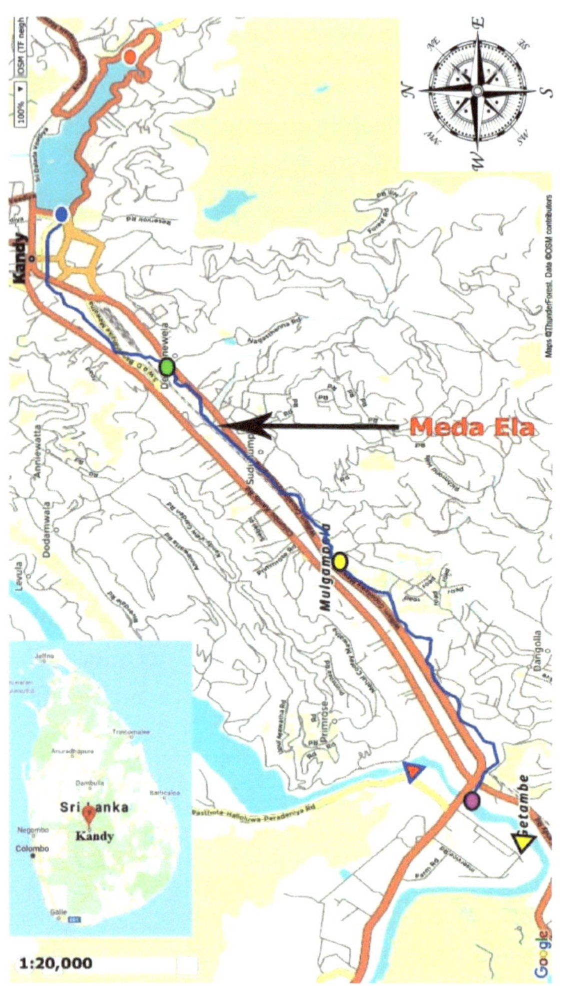

Figure 3.6 Site Map

Source: www.gpsvisualizer.com

3.2.3 Study area features

3.2.3.1 Geographical extent of the study area

Meda Ela which is 4.4 Km long is the main drainage path for the southern part of the city of Kandy. It commences from the spillway of the Kandy Lake, flows in a south westerly direction adjacent to the William Gopallawa Mawatha and discharges into the Mahaweli Ganga at Getambe.

The initial reach of the Meda Ela, from the spillway of the Kandy Lake to about 1.3 km, consists of two sections of underground conduits in the city centre area, and an open drain joining the two underground sections.

In the downstream area, the Meda Ela flows as an open drain close to the William Goppallawa Mawatha and the Railway line, crossing the William Gopallawa Mawatha and the railway line close to the discharge point at Getambe. Annex 01 shows end of the underground section near the Edmond Silva playground at Deiyannewela.

In the upstream reach of this drain section up to the William Goppallawa Mawatha Bridge, the drain runs through heavily built up areas, with structures forming along the banks of the drain. The railway line and the William Goppallawa Mawatha are on either side of the drain, and are very close near the bridge. Over 20 foot bridges crossings and 3 road crossings can be seen in this reach. The Meda Ela takes two sharp bends both sides of the William Goppallawa Mawatha Bridge.

Downstream of the bridge, the drain is around 2.5 km in length. In this reach, the first 1.7 km the banks are protected with Gabions, Rubble Masonry and concrete walls and the balance length the banks are unprotected.

3.2.3.2 Topography and terrain

Kandy City is a plateau in the central mountainous region and lies 462 to 489 MSL while canal lies in the range of 460m to 490m MSL The terrain is made up of a basin-like morphology and does not contain many steep, plunging slopes except in the surrounding mountains. The topography in this plateau consists of undulating plains with hillocks and valleys formed by the drainage paths. Topographically, the terrain of the watershed of the Meda Ela consists of rolling hills and valleys. A considerable number of perennial and seasonal tributaries originate from the hilly terrain empty into the main stream on either side of the canal.

3.2.3.3   Temperature

With Kandy located in the centre of the island and in a high elevation (488 metres above mean sea level), the city has a relatively wetter and cooler temperature than that of the tropical climate of the rest of the country, especially the coastal regions. Kandy's climate is tropical as mean temperatures year round are above 24.5^0C on average.

3.2.3.4   Soil Type

The soil cover mainly consisting of Reddish Brown Latosolic soils and loams made from the weathering of underlying rocks and boulders and rock outcrops. It is also located within a belt of Quartzite, quartz schist commonly with sillimanite adjacent to widespread area of Hornblende/Hornblende biotite gneiss.

The main geological feature of the Kandy City and its surrounding area is a band of marble that extends up to 650 m to one kilometre thick. This band is classified as coarse crystalline mainly made up of calcite. Calcsilicate gneiss intruded as bands within the host marble including scapolite and spinel as additional minerals. Collectively these two rock types give rise to red-brown overburden latosolic soil that on average ranges in thickness from one to three meters.

Geologically, the location where the canal lies is on highly weathered quartzite, crystalline marble and gneisses. For most of its course, the canal flows through a crystalline limestone bed. The alluvial bed of the stream in the unpaved areas is highly silted and the total amount of bed sediment is substantially higher towards the confluence of the canal with the main river at Getambe.

3.2.4 Selection of Water quality Parameters

The water quality parameters that were tested in selected monitoring locations are discussed under this topic. Parameters were selected to meet research objectives.

These include Temperature, Dissolved Oxygen, Biological Oxygen Demand, pH and Total Dissolved Solid. Following reasons are given in order to justify the selection of parameters.

3.2.4.1   Temperature

Temperature exerts a major influence on biological activity and growth. It governs the kinds of aquatic life that can live in the water. Fish, insects, zooplankton, phytoplankton, and other aquatic species all have a preferred temperature range. If temperatures get too far above or below this preferred range, the number of individuals of the species decreases until finally there are none. Temperature is also important because of its influence on water chemistry. The rate of chemical reactions generally increases at higher temperature, which in turn affects biological activity. An important example of the effects of temperature on water chemistry is its impact on oxygen. Warm water holds less oxygen than cool water, so it may be saturated with oxygen but still not contain enough for survival of aquatic life.

3.2.4.2   Dissolved Oxygen

Like terrestrial animals, fish and other aquatic organisms need oxygen to live. Like any other gas diffusion process, the transfer is efficient only above certain concentrations. So, a certain minimum amount of oxygen must be present in water for aquatic life to survive. Like any other gas diffusion process, the transfer is efficient only above certain concentrations. Therefore, a certain minimum amount of oxygen must be present in water for aquatic life to survive. In addition to being required by aquatic organisms for respiration, oxygen also is used for decomposition of organic matter and other biological and chemical processes.

3.2.4.3   pH

The pH of a sample of water is a measure of the concentration of hydrogen ions. The pH of water determines the solubility (amount that can be dissolved in the water) and biological availability (amount that can be utilized by aquatic life) of chemical constituents such as nutrients (phosphorus, nitrogen, and carbon) and heavy metals (lead, copper, cadmium, etc.). pH also determines whether aquatic life can use it. In the case of heavy metals, the degree to which they are soluble determines their toxicity. Metals tend to be more toxic at lower pH because they are more soluble (Michaud 1991).

3.2.4.4   Chemical Oxygen Demand

COD is an important water quality parameter because, similar to BOD, it provides an index to assess the effect discharged wastewater will have on the receiving environment. Higher COD levels mean a greater amount of oxidizable organic material in the sample, which will reduce dissolved oxygen (DO) levels. A reduction in DO can lead to anaerobic conditions, which is deleterious to higher aquatic life forms.

3.2.4.5   Biochemical Oxygen Demand

BOD provides an index to assess the effect discharged wastewater will have on the receiving environment. The higher the BOD value, the greater the amount of organic matter or "food" available for oxygen consuming bacteria. If the rate of DO consumption by bacteria exceeds the supply of DO from aquatic plants, algae photosynthesis or diffusing from air, unfavourable conditions occur. Depletion of DO causes stress on aquatic organisms, making the environment unsuitable for life. Further, dramatic depletion can lead to hypoxia or anoxic environments.

3.2.4.6   Total Dissolved Solid

Total dissolved solids (TDS) comprise inorganic salts (principally calcium, magnesium, potassium, sodium, bicarbonates, chlorides, and sulfates) and some small amounts of organic matter that are dissolved in water. In general, the total dissolved solids concentration is the sum of the cations (positively charged) and anions (negatively charged) ions in the water. Therefore, the total dissolved solids test provides a qualitative measure of the amount of dissolved ions. Therefore, the total dissolved solids test is used as an indicator test to determine the general quality of the water.

3.2.5 Sample collection

3.2.5.1   Cleanliness and storage of sampling equipment

Every effort was made to maintain a high degree of cleanliness for all equipment including bottles to assure that the analytical data are truly representative of the quality of the water at the time of sampling.

3.2.5.2   Collecting Samples

Each sample bottle was labelled with specific identification number in order to ensure that each monitoring location has each sample set.

(A)Sampling from Bank

When sampling from bank always collected samples while facing upstream. The bottles were filled one at a time. The bottle was uncapped immediately before sampling. While holding the cap in one hand, the bottle was slowly lowered into the water, with the opening facing downstream into the current, until the lower lip of the opening is just submerged. Allowed the water to fill the bottle very gradually, avoiding any turbulence. When the water level in the bottle has stabilized, slowly the bottle was turned upright and filled it completely. The bottle was kept under water and allowed it to overflow for 4 or 5 seconds to ensure that no air bubbles are trapped. The bottle was capped while it was still submerged. Then the bottle was lifted out of water.

(B)Bridge Sampling

The free end of the rope was tied to the bridge railing to secure the sampler. Sampler was swung as far upstream as possible before releasing it from the upstream side of the bridge.

3.2.5.3   Reagent Application

Certain water samples required reagent application (For DO and BOD test). Prior to reagent application, protective disposable gloves were put on. The reagent was poured into its designated sample bottle and re-capped the bottle. Invert the water sample bottle several times to mix reagent with sample water.

3.2.6 Sample testing

In-situ testing was carried out for some parameters while some are tested in the laboratory.

3.2.6.1   Temperature

Temperature was measured by placing the thermometer in the sampling container and allowed the thermometer time to come to equilibrium and read immediately.

3.2.6.2   pH

The pH electrode was thoroughly rinsed between measurements with distilled water to prevent carryover contamination of the tested samples. Afterwards the electrode was gently blotted on a cleaning tissue to remove the excess rinse water. The pH electrode was dipped into a testing sample and stirred it. The pH was completed when the pH reading was stable.

3.2.6.3   Dissolved Oxygen

In-situ testing was carried out using a dissolved oxygen meter. However in order to make sure the accuracy of readings, the sample was tested again in the laboratory.

Winkler method was performed as the laboratory testing technique. Dissolved oxygen levels in sample bottles change quickly due to the decomposition of organic material by microorganisms or the production of oxygen by algae and other plants in the sample. This will lower the DO reading. Therefore it is required to "fix" the sample in the field and then deliver it to a lab for titration. Immediately after the sample was collected the stopper was removed and added the fixing reagents to the sample. Immediately the stopper was inserted so air was not trapped in the bottle and inverted several times to mix. a few minutes was waited until the flock in the solution had settled. Again the bottle was inverted several times and waited until the flock had settled. This ensured complete reaction of the sample and reagents.

The following procedure was followed to determine the quantity of dissolved oxygen in a fixed sample:

- ✓ Water samples were collected to be tested in test tubes. The tubes were filled completely, holding the tube horizontally and gently lowering it through the water surface. Then the tubes were stoppered.
- ✓ With a Barrel-type pipet, 6 drops of Winkler solution #1 (manganous sulfate solution) were directly added to the sample tube, holding the pipet tip as close to the sample surface as possible. With a second pipet, 6 drops of Winkler solution #2 (alkaline-iodide solution) were added in the same fashion. The tube was stoppered and inverted several times to mix. This step fixes, or sequesters, the dissolved oxygen in the sample.
- ✓ Allowed the precipitate formed and to settle to about one half the volume of the tube.
- ✓ 6–7 drops of concentrated sulfuric acid were added to each sample tube, stoppered and inverted several times to mix. The acid solubilized the precipitate, giving a clear, yellow-gold solution.
- ✓ 20 mL from the sample tube was transferred into a 125-mL conical flask
- ✓ The burette was filled with the sodium thiosulfate solution. The sample was titrated in the flask with the sodium thiosulfate solution in the burette until the sample fades to a pale straw colour.
- ✓ 6 drops of starch solution was added to the flask and swirled to mix. The sample will turn dark purple-blue. Titrating was continued with the sodium thiosulfate solution to the colourless endpoint.
- ✓ The total number of millilitres of sodium thiosulfate dispensed from the burette was recorded. This value is directly proportional to the amount of oxygen dissolved in the original sample. Millilitres (mL) of sodium thiosulfate used equals dissolved oxygen concentration in milligrams per liter (mg/L).

3.2.6.4   Biochemical Oxygen Demand

Previous procedure for DO determination was used to measure the initial dissolved oxygen concentration (mg/L) in each sample. Each sample in then was placed into a dark incubator at 20°C for five days. After five days the DO determination procedure was conducted again to measure a final dissolved oxygen concentration. The final DO reading was then subtracted from the initial DO reading and the result was BOD concentration (mg/L) of the sample.

3.2.6.5   Chemical oxygen demand

The open reflux method was used in order to determine COD level of samples because it is suitable for a wide range of wastes where a large sample size is preferred. Principle of this method is by refluxing the sample in strongly acid solution with a known excess of potassium dichromate ($K_2Cr_2O_7$) most types of organic matter are oxidized. After digestion, the remaining unreduced $K_2Cr_2O_7$ is titrated with ferrous ammonium sulphate to determine the amount of K2Cr2O7 consumed and the oxidizable matter is calculated in terms of oxygen equivalent. The following procedure was followed to determine the level of Chemical oxygen demand in the samples.

- ✓ Sample was pipetted 50.00 mL into a 500-mL refluxing flask.
- ✓ Initially 1 g of $HgSO_4$, several glass beads was added to the flask and very slowly 5.0 mL of sulphuric acid reagent was added with mixing to dissolve $HgSO_4$.
- ✓ 25.00 mL of 0.04167M $K_2Cr_2O_7$ solution was added and mixed it.
- ✓ Flask was attached to condenser and turned on cooling water and remaining sulphuric acid reagent (70 mL) was added through open end of condenser. (swirling and mixing was continued while adding sulphuric acid reagent)
- ✓ Open end of condenser was covered with a small beaker to prevent foreign material from entering refluxing mixture and refluxed for 2 h.
- ✓ Then condenser was cooled and washed down with distilled water
- ✓ Reflux condenser was disconnected and diluted mixture to about twice its volume with distilled water.
- ✓ Solution was cooled to room temperature and titrated excess $K_2Cr_2O_7$ with ferrous ammonium sulphate (FAS), using 0.10 to 0.15 mL (2 to 3 drops) ferroin indicator.

- ✓ As the end point of the titration was taken the first sharp colour change from blue-green to reddish brown that persists for 1 min or longer.
- ✓ In the same manner, a blank containing the reagents and a volume of distilled water equal to that of sample was refluxed and titrated.

Calculation was carried out as per following equation.

$$\text{COD as mg O2/L} = \frac{(A-B)*M*8000}{mL\ Sample}$$

Where:

A is mL FAS used for blank,
B is mL FAS used for sample,
M is molarity of FAS, and
8000 milliequivalent weight of oxygen 1000 mL/L.

3.2.6.6 Total Dissolved Solids

In order to measure Total Dissolved Solids of the samples, Gravimetric method was used. Total dissolved solids is a measure of the dissolved matter in a water that remains after all the water has been evaporated. Principle of this method is a known volume of a well-mixed sample is filtered through a standard glass-fiber filter and the filtrate collected. The filtrate is evaporated to a constant weight condition in an oven maintained at a temperature of 180°C to remove mechanically occluded water. The mass of the dried sample's dissolved solids is determined and used to calculate the concentration of total dissolved solids in the sample. Following procedure was carried out in order for determination of TDS.

- ✓ A sample evaporating dish was prepared by ensuring that it was cleaned and did not contain residue from a previous use. In order to do that the inside surface of the evaporating dish was rinsed with approximately 5 mL of concentrated hydrochloric acid and rinsed all surfaces of the evaporating dish using first tap water and then using deionized or distilled water for the final cleansing rinse
- ✓ The clean evaporating dish was dried in a convention oven at a temperature of $180 \pm 2°C$ for 01hr.
- ✓ Then cleaned dish was cooled and dry to room temperature and weigh and recorded its weight.
- ✓ A glass-fiber filter was prepared by placing and centering a filter disk onto the filter support screen of the filtration apparatus and attached the funnel.

✓ Moderate vacuum was applied and rinsed the filter with three successive volumes of 30 mL distilled water and left the vacuum on until all traces of water have been removed from the filter.

✓ A volume of well-mixed sample was transferred onto the filter by using a pipet with the vacuum applied.

✓ The entire volume of sample filtrate was transferred and rinse water to a pre-weighed dish and recorded the total volume of sample added.

✓ The sample was evaporated in an oven at a temperature of 80°C to remove the free-standing water.

✓ The sample was dried in an oven at a temperature of 180°C for 01 hr.

✓ The dish containing the sample was removed from the oven, cooling it to room temperature and then weighed it. This was recorded as the first weight.

✓ The drying cycle was repeated for 01 hr. and again cool, weigh and record as the second weight.

✓ The weight change was calculated between the first and second weights,

CHAPTER FOUR: DATA PRESENTATION AND ANALYSIS

4.1 Assessment of the current water quality condition of Meda Ela-Kandy

Water quality monitoring was carried out in selected locations in dry season and wet season of 2018. Following tables show the water quality monitoring results of each season.

Table 4.1 Monitoring results of Water Samples Collected in wet season (October 2018)

Parameters	Unit	ME1	ME2	ME3	ME4	ME5	MR1	MR2
Temperature	^{o}C	24.6	24.1	25.4	26.8	25.1	24.3	23.9
pH	-	8.25	8.57	7.1	7.7	8.07	7.4	7.3
TDS	mg/l	216	198	181	153	226	39	38
DO	mg/l	5.03	6.24	5.7	5.2	7.26	7.6	6.9
COD	mg/l	57	14	65	20	7	11	8
BOD 5	mg/l	11.7	3.7	5.9	12	2.7	6	8

Source: Prepared by Author

Table 4.2 Monitoring results of Water Samples Collected in dry season (February 2018)

Parameters	Unit	ME1	ME2	ME3	ME4	ME5	MR1	MR2
Temperature	^{o}C	25.4	25.1	26.2	27.8	26.6	28.6	27.4
pH	-	7.14	7.69	7.11	7.2	7.08	7.5	7.6
TDS	mg/l	230	205	250	330	264	80	80
DO	mg/l	7.3	7.9	5.7	1.8	2.8	4.7	4.9
COD	mg/l	47	27	29	92	48	19	18
BOD 5	mg/l	4.2	2.2	2.4	55	40	1.6	2.4

Source: Prepared by Author

Following figures demonstrate the Dissolved Oxygen variation with the temperature of Meda Ela in each monitoring session. In addition to seasonal variations in water temperature caused by changing air temperatures, many other physical aspects cause variation in temperature. Velocity also influences temperature. A particle of water in a fast-moving canal is exposed to sunlight for a shorter time than that in a slow-moving canal.

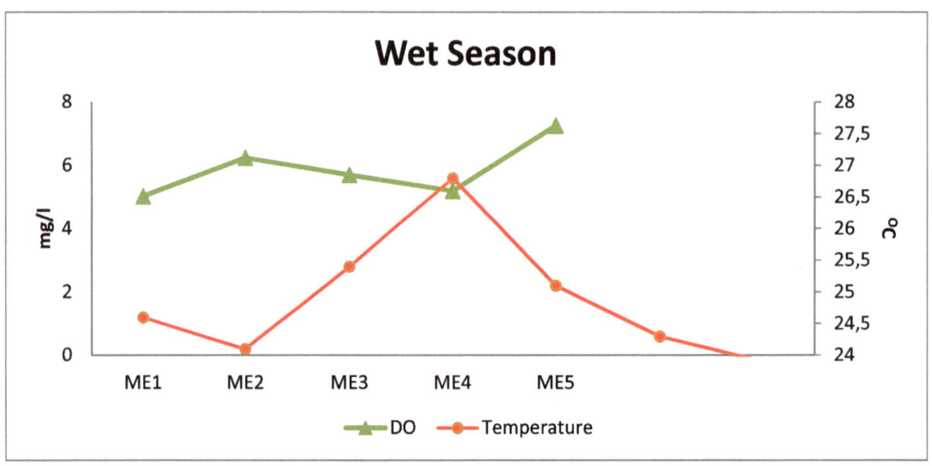

Figure 4.1 Variation of Dissolved Oxygen with the temperature in wet season along in the Meda Ela (Source: prepared by Author)

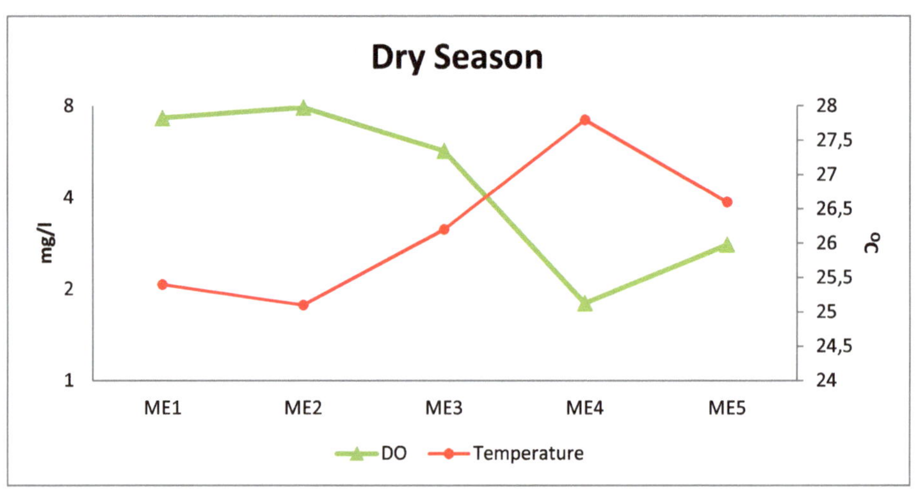

Figure 4.2 Variation of Dissolved Oxygen with the temperature in dry season along in the Meda Ela (Source: prepared by Author)

A physical process that impacts DO concentrations has to do with the temperature of the water. Cold water can hold more gas than warm water and it is proved by the correlations that depicts in figure 4.1 and figure 4.2. As per the results, temperature and DO concentration of the water have shown an inverse correlation. For instance in both seasons, from ME2 to ME4 we can observe a gradual increase in temperature and temperature drop at ME5. On the other hand, a gradual drop in DO concentration is shown from ME2 to ME4 and ME5 shows comparatively high DO concentration.

Other than the temperature pollution tends to cause a decrease in dissolved oxygen concentrations. This change can be caused by addition of effluent or runoff water with a low concentration of DO or chemical or biological constituents that is they require large amounts of oxygen before they can be thoroughly decomposed.

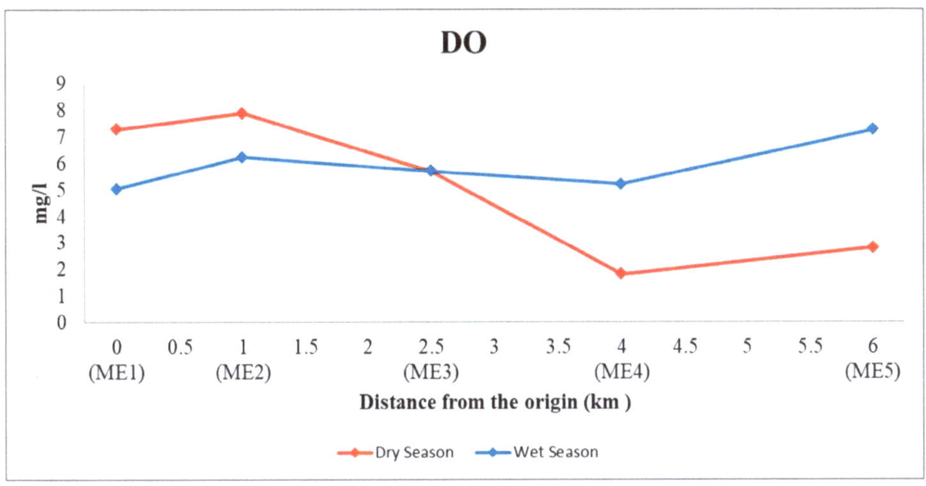

Figure 4.3 Variation of Dissolved Oxygen along in the Meda Ela (Source: prepared by Author)

When we consider the variation of Dissolved Oxygen separately in both seasons, we can identify a noticeable DO reduction at Heeressagala Junction (ME4) (Figure 4.3) and a mild improvement can be observed at the end of the canal. However, the overall variation shows deterioration in dissolved oxygen concentration in both seasons.

BOD and COD results were taken in to account in order to determine the individual contribution of biological and chemical constituents for the pollution. BOD is the amount of dissolved oxygen required by aerobic biological organisms to break down organic material in water and COD is the amount of dissolved oxygen required to break down organic as well as inorganic matter in water.

We can observe high concentration of BOD at Heeressagala junction (ME4) in both seasons (Figure 4.4). That is the most prominent feature of BOD variation of Meda Ela. Wet season shows rather incline in BOD concentrations within first 4km, but once Meda ela reaches Mahaweli River or at the end of the canal it demonstrates slight improvement. Although, BOD variation of the dry season exhibits similar pattern as wet season we can identify a significant escalation at the ME4 and it reduces towards the end of the canal but the intensity of BOD reduction is low. The BOD value in the dry season at the end of the canal is higher than the

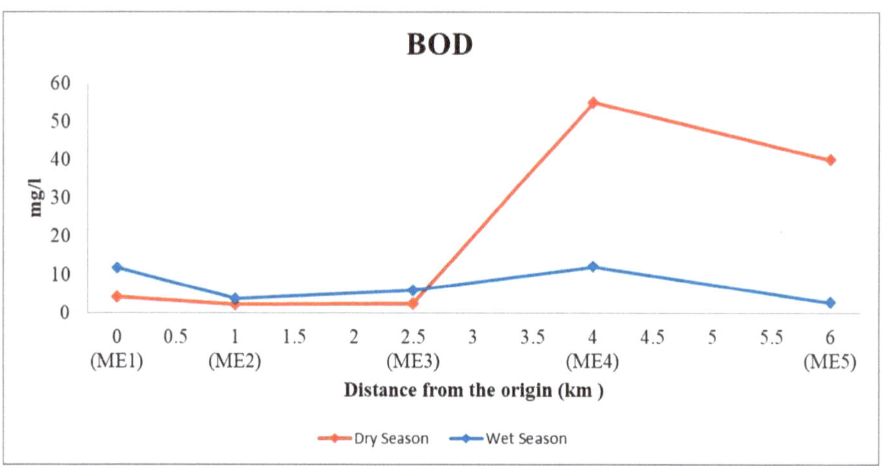

Figure 4.4 Variation of BOD along in the Meda Ela (Source: prepared by Author)

COD concentrations in Meda Ela fluctuate over the year (Figure 4.5) and same as BOD variation it exhibits reduction at the end of the canal. As usual highest concentration of COD is reported at ME4 in the dry season. However in the wet season, highest COD concentration can be found at ME3. Most probable reason of this high COD level at ME3 might be the inflow that comes from Kandy hospital premises especially during the rainy period.

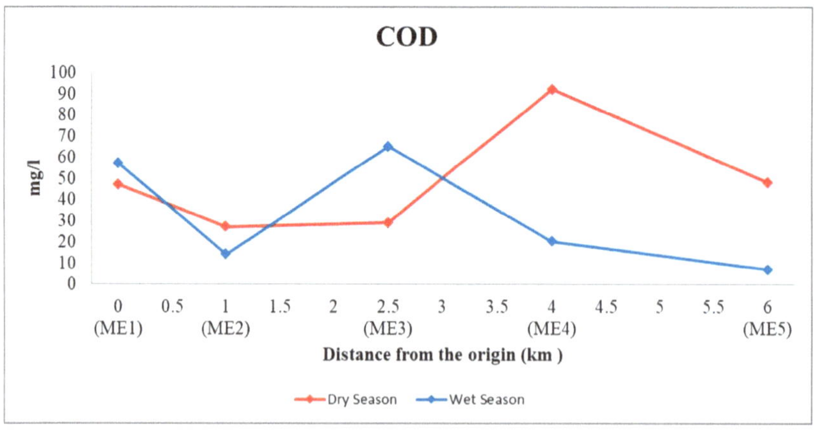

Figure 4.5 Variations of COD along in the Meda Ela (Source: prepared by Author)

For Total Dissolved Solids (TDS), the highest TDS value (330mg/l) of the canal was reported at Heeressagala Junction (ME4) in the dry season and it indicates the presence of high concentration of ionic salts. However, in the wet season highest TDS value was found at the end of the canal (Figure 4.6). Basically from the upstream to downstream TDS shows increasing trend in both seasons.

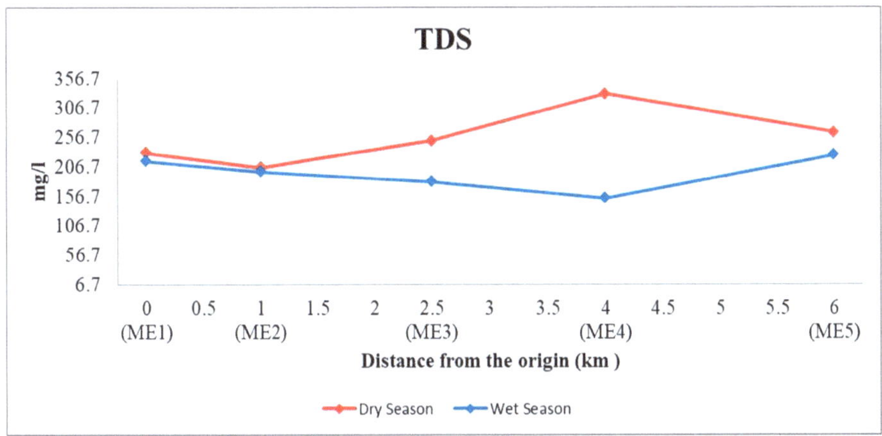

Figure 4.6 Variations of TDS along in the Meda Ela (Source: prepared by Author)

As per the results the pH values varied in the range 7.1 – 8.5 (Figure 4.7). The variation of pH shows similar pattern in both dry and wet seasons. But pH level of the wet season varies in a relatively high pH range.

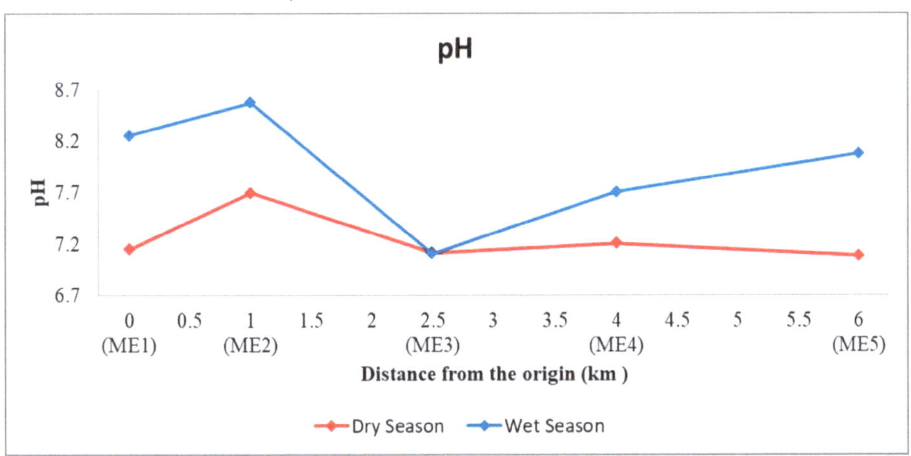

Figure 4.7 Variations of pH along in the Meda Ela (Source: prepared by Author)

4.2 Determination of the pollution level fluctuation of Meda Ela and Mahaweli River over the year

The water quality monitoring has been carried out for six different physiochemical parameters and the output of the monitoring consists with raw data that do not reflect a clear picture out of it. Therefore a method that helps to understand the collective contribution of physiochemical parameter for the pollution had to be selected. Once the data would be generalized, it is easy to ascertain the pollution level of each location. Determination of magnitude of the pollution at each monitoring location would assist to fabricate a precise correlation. Since the water quality index is used to generalize water quality monitoring data, it was decided to develop a Water Quality Index and calculate the magnitude of the pollution of each monitoring location.

4.2.1 Water Quality Index (WQI)

The WQI was first introduced by Horton in the early 1970s; it is a representation of the mathematical means of calculating a single value from many test results. The resulted index represents the level of water quality in a given water area, such as ponds, lake, river or stream (Al-Mashagbah, 2015).

The objective of water quality index is to change the complexity of the water quality data into information that can be used easily by the public. A single number is not enough to describe all of water quality parameters that are not included in the index. On the other hand, a water quality index based on some very important parameters can provide a single indicator of water quality.

In formulation of water quality index the relative importance of various parameters depends on intended use of water. Mostly it is done from the point of view of its suitability for human consumption. However in this case since Meda-Ela is a polluted canal and people do not consume its water directly, WQI calculations are done from the perspective of its environmental impact.

4.2.2 WQI Calculation

Calculation of WQI was carried out in this work by Horton's method. The WQI is calculated by using the expression given in Equation (4.1).

$$WQI = \frac{\sum q_n\, W_n}{\sum W_n}$$

$$(4.1)$$

Where, q_n = Quality rating of nth water quality parameter.

W_n = Unit weight of nth water quality parameter.

4.2.2.1 Quality rating (q_n)

The quality rating (q_n) is calculated using the expression given in Equation (4.2).

$$q_n = \left[\frac{(V_n - V_{id})}{(S_n - V_{id})}\right] X100 \qquad (4.2)$$

Where, V_n = Observed value of nth water quality parameter at a given sample location.

V_{id} = Ideal value for n^{th} parameter in pure water.

In most cases $V_{id} = 0$ except in certain parameters like pH, dissolved oxygen etc.,

Calculation of quality rating for pH & DO $(V_{id} \neq 0)$

$$q_{pH} = \left[\frac{(V_{pH} - 7.0)}{(S_{pH} - 7.0)}\right] X100$$

$$q_{DO} = \left[\frac{(V_{DO} - 14.6)}{(S_{DO} - 14.6)}\right] X100$$

S_n = Standard permissible value of nth water quality parameter.

4.2.2.2 Unit weight

The unit weight (W_n) is calculated using the expression given in Equation (4.3).

$$W_n = \frac{k}{S_n}$$

$$(4.3)$$

Where,

S_n = Standard permissible value of nth water quality parameter.

k = Constant of proportionality and it is calculated by using the expression given in Equation (4.4).

$$k = \frac{1}{\sum 1/S_{n=1,2...n}}$$

(4.4)

4.2.2.3 Standard values and unit weights of water quality parameters

The water quality parameters are selected based on its direct involvement in deteriorating water quality. The standards for discharge of effluents into inland surface waters, recommended by National Environmental (Protection and Quality) Regulations No.1 of 1990 and Proposed Ambient Water Quality Standards for Inland Waters Sri Lanka Parameter Unit (CEA/SLSI 2001) are considered for the computation of quality rating (q_n) and unit weights (W_n).

For the purpose of calculation of WQI for the study area, five water quality parameters have been selected. They are pH, TDS, DO, BOD, COD. The values of these parameters are found high above the permissible limits in some of the samples of the study area. The higher values of these parameters would increase WQI value. The standard values of water quality parameters and their corresponding ideal values and unit weights are given in Table 4.3.

Table 4.3 Standard values of water quality parameters and their corresponding ideal values and unit weights

No	Parameters	S_n	Ideal Value (V_{id})	k Value	Unit Weight (W_n)
1	pH	8.5	7	1.299	0.153
2	TDS	500	0	1.299	0.003
3	DO	3	14.6	1.299	0.433
4	BOD	4	0	1.299	0.087
5	COD	15	0	1.299	0.325

Source: prepared by Author

4.2.3 WQI of study area

The WQI values of the study area for wet and dry season samples were calculated separately. Table 4.4 below gives the calculation of WQI of the Inflow from Ampitiya (ME1) in wet season as an example.

Table 4.4 Calculation of WQI of the Inflow from Ampitiya (ME1)

Parameter	Observed value V_n	Unit weight W_n	Quality rating q_n	$q_n W_n$
pH	8.25	0.153	83.33	12.738
TDS	216	0.003	43.2	0.112
DO	5.03	0.433	82.5	35.731
COD	57	0.087	380	32.916
BOD 5	11.7	0.325	292.5	95.011
		$\sum W_n = 1$		$\sum q_n W_n = 176.50$

Source: prepared by Author

The water quality index (WQI) of Inflow from Ampitiya was then calculated using the weighted arithmetic index formula as follows.

$$WQI = \frac{\sum q_n W_n}{\sum W_n} = \frac{176.50}{1} = \mathbf{176.50}$$

Table 4.5 Calculated WQI values of each location in wet and dry season

Wet Season		Dry Season	
Location	WQI	Location	WQI
ME1	176.51	ME1	90.05
ME2	85.45	ME2	65.61
ME3	119.79	ME3	70.72
ME4	151.31	ME4	316.50
ME5	91.19	ME5	104.37
MR1	85.31	MR1	51.17
MR2	101.41	MR2	61.25

Source: prepared by Author

Fluctuation of WQI of Meda Ela and Mahaweli River in wet season and dry season exhibits similar pattern.

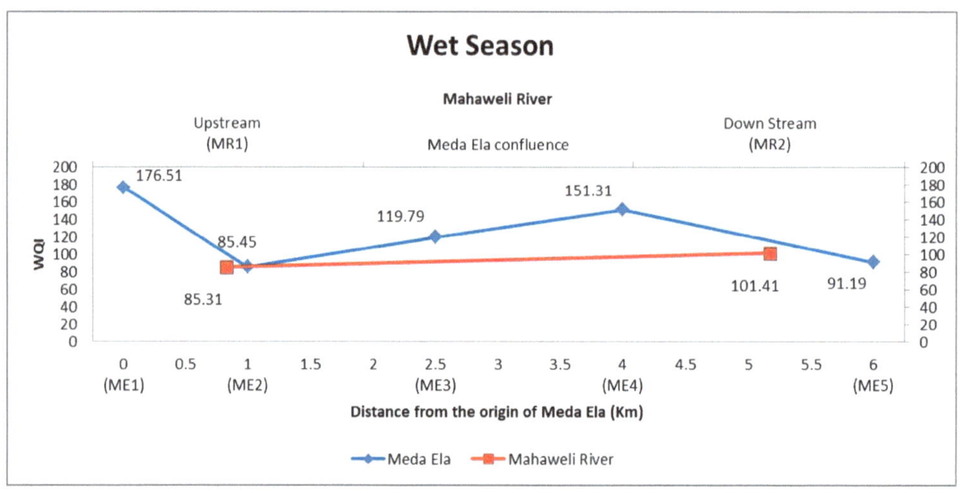

Figure 4.8: Variation of the WQI in wet season

Source: prepared by Author

Figure 4.9: Variation of the WQI in dry season

Source: prepared by Author

In both wet season and dry season ME1 shows high WQI value rather than ME2 and ME3. The most probable reason of this observation might be the run off and unauthorised discharging of commercial and domestic establishments that locate in Ampitiya area. This is proved by the WQI of ME1 in wet season because it is comparatively higher than dry season.

Relatively ME2 shows low WQI value than ME1 in both seasons, which means slight improvement in water quality could be observed at the outflow of Kandy Lake. However from ME2 to ME4 gradual deterioration can be observed. Nevertheless, a rapid increase in pollution level is recorded in dry season at ME4. But at the time of sample collection, a flow of black water could be found at the particular location. That unauthorized discharging might be the reason for the exceptional WQI value which recorded at ME4 in dry season. However, ME4 has shown significant pollution level comparatively other monitoring locations of Meda Ela in both seasons. Heeressagala is the most congested area that is passed by Meda Ela. Consequently a high level pollution is taken place due to unauthorized waste discharging and urban runoff.

Meanwhile, a gradual decrease in the pollution level could be identified toward the ME5 in both seasons. Even though ME4 shows significant pollution level, it has been decreased when Meda Ela reaches Mahaweli River due to the significant distance (2.0 Km) from Heeressagala Junction to Meda Ela confluence and there is no significant point source pollution that can be identified.

When we consider WQI fluctuation of Mahaweli River, it exhibits same pattern in both seasons which is high WQI value at downstream rather than upstream. However, overall water quality of the Mahaweli River in wet season remains as poor.

4.3 Confirmation of the impact on Mahaweli River from Meda Ela.

In accordance with the figure 4.8 and figure 4.9, the pollution level of Mahaweli River is recorded as comparatively high in wet season and also a deterioration of water quality can be observed toward the downstream in both seasons. But the intensity of that deterioration is comparatively high in wet season than dry season. In wet season, when we compare WQIs of Meda Ela confluence, upstream and downstream of Mahaweli River, we can see that Mahaweli River shows rapid increase of WQI even though comparatively low WQI value that recorded at Meda Ela confluence. And also in dry season Meda Ela confluence shows comparative high WQI value but Mahaweli River does not show rapid WQI increasing toward the downstream. Evidently, this WQI variation does not prove that Meda Ela has significant potential that can pollute Mahaweli River. But it does not mean that Meda Ela does not contribute to the pollution of Mahaweli River at all. Meda Ela may affects Mahaweli River to a certain extent but other than the Meda Ela, some point source and nonpoint source pollution such as run-off and unauthorized discharging may results increasing of WQI from upstream to downstream of Mahaweli River.

CHAPTER FIVE: SUMMARY AND CONCLUSION

5.1 WQI and status

The ranges of WQI and the corresponding status of water quality are summarized in table 5.1

Table 5.1 WQI and corresponding water quality status.

WQI	Status
0 – 25	Excellent
25 – 50	Good
51 -75	Fair
76 – 100	Poor
101 -150	Very Poor
Above 150	Unfit for Fish and aquatic life

Source: Boah *et al*, 2015

In accordance with the above criteria, WQI of each season was categorized as follows.

Table 5.2 WQI of the Wet season samples and Dry season samples

WQI	Status	Representing Wet season samples	Representing Dry season samples
0 – 25	Excellent	-	-
25 – 50	Good	-	-
51 -75	Fair	-	ME2,ME3,MR1,MR2
76 – 100	Poor	ME2,ME5,MR1	ME1
101 -150	Very Poor	ME3,MR2	ME5
Above 150	Unfit	ME1,ME4	ME4

Source: prepared by Author

As per Table 5.2 ME1 shows unfit water quality condition in wet season. Even so, it has shown mild improvement in water quality during the dry season. However there is a significant difference between WQI values of wet season and dry season. In wet season it was recorded the WQI value of ME1 as 176.51. And a significant reduction of the WQI value could be identified in dry season (90.05).

WQI of ME2 which was recorded as "Poor" in wet season, reflects an improvement in dry season since it had been changed into "Fair" water quality status. Same as ME1 and ME2, WQI of ME3 shows an improvement in dry season.

When we consider WQI of ME4, it remains in "Unfit" condition in both wet and dry season. Notwithstanding, water quality of most of the locations in Meda Ela had shown an improvement in dry season, ME5 shows a water quality deterioration in dry season compared to the wet season.

Water quality of Mahaweli River shows significant difference between wet season and dry season. Higher deterioration rate can be observed in water quality in wet season.

5.2 Conclusion

WQI fluctuation of Meda Ela manifests same pattern over the year, but the intensity of the pollution is strong in wet season. And also average pollution level of the Meda ela in wet season is higher than dry season. Basically ME4 is the most polluted location in both seasons. However most prominent feature of this fluctuation is reduction of pollution level toward the Meda Ela confluence soon after it passes Heeressagala junction. This phenomenon can be noted in both seasons. Notwithstanding this rapid decline, Meda Ela shows gradual increase of water quality deterioration from origin to its discharge point in dry season while it exhibits mild improvement toward the confluence in wet season. Nevertheless, the overall pollution status of the Meda Ela in wet season is higher than dry season. The results of the study reflect considerable water pollution in Kandy Lake, Meda Ela and in Mahaweli River mainly because sewage in the downtown area flows directly into drainage system and then into Meda Ela. However during the study we could not identify clear relationship between Meda Ela and Mahaweli River water pollution.

Basically Kandy Lake and Meda Ela demonstrate high pollution level and it fluctuates. However, none of the water quality parameters that were measured at the Meda Ela confluence has exceeded the general standard for the discharge of wastewater into inland surface waters. Notwithstanding this water quality improvement in Meda Ela confluence, Mahaweli River shows water quality deterioration toward the downstream. On the other hand, as per the EIA study which was conducted by Kandy City Wastewater Management Project the flow of the Mahaweli River is about $122,900m^3/$ day at the median equivalent to more than 100 times the flow of Meda Ela. Consequently, we can figure out that other than the Meda Ela , there might be several other point or non-point source pollution that contribute to pollution of the Mahaweli River.

The pollution of the Kandy Lake, spread of Algae blooms covering a major part of the lake, flow of pollutant in Meda Ela , and pollution of River water are major environmental problems in Kandy.

In order to minimize the water pollution there should be a proper pollution management mechanism. Following section discusses the possibilities of the management strategies that can be adopted to minimize the surface water pollution in Meda Ela and Mahaweli River.

5.2.1 Management strategies that prevent/minimise water pollution of Meda Ela and Mahaweli River

The goals of urban water management should be to ensure access to water and sanitation infrastructure and services; manage rainwater, wastewater, storm water drainage, and runoff pollution. Rather than proposing a set of quick fixes for isolated urban water management problems it should reframe a city's relationships to water and other resources, and reconceptualises the ways in which they can be overseen.

Due to limitation of space, individual septic tanks and soakage pits are not properly operated or maintained overcrowded areas. Since the city does not have wastewater treatment system this sewer is dumped not only into Meda Ela but also into Mahaweli River and Kandy Lake especially during the rain. Therefore in order to overcome this issue the city should be facilitated with common wastewater treatment system. Other than a centralized wastewater treatment facility there should be well function separate wastewater treatment systems in the critical institutes like hospitals in order to treat clinical wastewater. Currently Kandy and Peradeniya hospitals have such treatment systems. But water quality of the Meda Ela does not reflect the contribution of those facilities since probably due to improper operation and maintenance. A regular water quality monitoring of the effluent should be carried out in order to ensure the functioning of these wastewater systems.

One of the main reasons of the water pollution is the poverty. Generally, most low income families do not have proper sanitary facilities which they can afford. Consequently they tend to use low cost sanitary methods instead of acceptable practices. Therefore such low income families should be identified and they should be encouraged to use proper sanitary system by supporting subsidy or required materials.

As a simultaneous effort, community awareness should be enhanced under many different forms such as: Communication and education for people to improve their knowledge, deep understanding of the importance of the use of water for the environment and human, and implement education program for protecting the water environment in the school. This is long-term strategy and the most effective

REFERENCES

Abdullah, A. M., & Hussona, E. D. (2014). Water Quality Assessment of Mahmoudia Canal in Northern West of Egypt. *Journal of Pollution Effects & Control, 02*(02), 121.

Abeygunawardana, A., Dayawansa, N., & Pathmarajha, S. (2009). Population pressure and unplanned waste disposal on water quality of an urban stream: A case study of Meda Ela Catchment, Kandy, Sri Lanka. In *the Fourth South Asia Water Conference, Interfacing poverty, livelihood and climate change in water resources development: Lessons in South Asia* (pp. 311-323).

Abeygunawardane, A., Dayawansa, N., & Pathmarajha, S. (2011). Socioeconomic Implications of Water Pollution in an Urban Environment A Case Study in *Meda Ela* Catchment, Kandy, Sri Lanka. *Tropical Agricultural Research, 22*(4), 374.

Abeysinghe, P. K. (2007). *Willingness to pay for wastewater disposal by commercial water users in Kandy municipality* (Unpublished master's thesis). University of Peradeniya, Sri Lanka.

Adachi, K., & Tainosho, Y. (2005). Single particle characterization of size-fractionated road sediments. *Applied Geochemistry, 20*(5), 849-859.

Allison, R., Chiew, F., & McMahon, T. (1998). Nutrient contribution of leaf litter in urban stormwater. *Journal of Environmental Management, 54*(4), 269-272.

Al-Mashagbah, A. F. (2015). Assessment of Surface Water Quality of King Abdullah Canal, Using Physico-Chemical Characteristics and Water Quality Index, Jordan. *Journal of Water Resource and Protection, 07*(04), 339-352.

Al-Mashagbah, A. F. (2015). Assessment of Surface Water Quality of King Abdullah Canal, Using Physico-Chemical Characteristics and Water Quality Index, Jordan. *Journal of Water Resource and Protection, 07*(04), 339-352.

Anhwange, B. A., Agbaji, E. B., & Gimba, E. C. (2012). Impact assessment of human activities and seasonal variation on River Benue, within Makurdi Metropolis. *Int. J. Sci. Technol, 2*, 248-259.

Aull, M. E. (2005). *Water quality indicators in watershed sub basins with multiple lands uses* (Unpublished master's thesis). Faculty of Worcester Polytechnic institute.

Bannerman, R. T., Owens, D. W., Dodds, R. B., & Hornewer, N. J. (1993). Sources of Pollutants in Wisconsin Stormwater. *Water Science and Technology*, *28*(3-5), 241-259.

Beckwith, P., Ellis, J., Revitt, D., & Oldfield, F. (1986). Heavy metal and magnetic relationships for urban source sediments. *Physics of the Earth and Planetary Interiors*, *42*(1-2), 67-75.

Boah, D. K., Twum, S. B., & Pelig-Ba, K. B. (2015). Mathematical computation of water quality index of Vea dam in upper east Region of Ghana. *Environmental Sciences*, *3*, 11-16.

Brinkmann, W. (1985). Urban stormwater pollutants: Sources and loadings. *GeoJournal*, *11*(3).

Chapman, D. V. (1992). *Water Quality Assessments: A guide to the use of biota, sediments and water in environmental monitoring,*. Boca Raton, FL: CRC Press.

Chapman, D. V., & Kimstach, V. (1996). Selection of water quality variables. In *Water Quality Assessments: A guide to the use of biota, sediments and water in environmental monitoring* (2nd ed.). Published on behalf of UNESCO, WHO and UNEP.

Cordery, I. (1977). Quality characteristics of urban storm water in Sydney, Australia. *Water Resources Research*, *13*(1), 197-202.

Eaton, A. D., Baird, R. B., & Rice, E. W. (Eds.). (2017). *Standard Methods for the Examination of Water and Wastewater* (23rd ed.). American Public Health Association,Washington, DC.

Ellis, J. B., Revitt, D. M., & Llewellyn, N. (1997). Transport and the Environment: Effects of Organic Pollutants on Water Quality. *Water and Environment Journal*, *11*(3), 170-177.

Evans, J. J. (1997). Rubber Tire Leachates in the Aquatic Environment. *Reviews of Environmental Contamination and Toxicology*, 67-115.

Farahmand, T., Fleming, S. W., & Quilty, E. J. (2007). Detection and visualization of storm hydrograph changes under urbanization: An impulse response approach. *Journal of Environmental Management*, *85*(1), 93-100.

Fulcher, G. (1994). Urban stormwater quality from a residential catchment. *Science of The Total Environment*, *146-147*, 535-542.

Gajanayake, P., Perera, A. C., Pelpitiya, S. K., Jayasiri, C. N., Perera, D. D., Saumyarathna, G. R., … Kirinde, W. K. (2015). Effect of Urbanization on Temporal & Spatial Varition of Dissolved Oxygen Concentration in a Natural Stream: A Case Study In Meda-Ela Canal, Kandy, Sri Lanka. *International Research Symposium on Engineering Advancements*.

Goonetilleke, A., Thomas, E., Ginn, S., & Gilbert, D. (2005). Understanding the role of land use in urban stormwater quality management. *Journal of Environmental Management, 74*(1), 31-42.

Grattan, S. R. (2002). *Irrigation Water Salinity and Crop Production*. CA: University of California, Davis.

Gunawardana, T. K. (2011). *Influence of Physical & Chemical Properties of Solids on Heavy Metal Adsorption* (Doctoral dissertation, QUEENSLAND UNIVERSITY OF TECHNOLOGY).

Harrafi, H., Khedri, M., & Karaminejad, K. (2012). Determination of Chemical Oxygen Demand in Spent Caustic by Potentiometric Determination. *World Academy of Science, Engineering and Technology, 6*(7), 190-192.

Herngren, L., Goonetilleke, A., & Ayoko, G. A. (2006). Analysis of heavy metals in road-deposited sediments. *Analytica Chimica Acta, 571*(2), 270-278. doi:10.1016/j.aca.2006.04.064

Ileperuma, O. A. (2000). Environmental pollution in Sri Lanka: a review. *Journal of the National Science Foundation of Sri Lanka, 28*(4), 301.

James, W., & Shivalingaiah, B. (1985). Storm water pollution modelling: buildup of dust and dirt on surfaces subject to runoff. *Canadian Journal of Civil Engineering, 12*(4), 906-915.

Jinadasa, K. B., Wijewardena, S. K., Zhang, D. Q., Gersberg, R. M., Kalpage, C. S., Tan, S. K., … Ng, W. J. (2012). Socio-Environmental Impact of Water Pollution on the Mid-canal (Meda Ela), Sri Lanka. *Journal of Water Resource and Protection, 04*(07), 451-459.

Liston, P., & Maher, W. (1997). Water quality for maintenance of aquatic ecosystems: appropriate indicators and analysis. *Australia:State of the Environment Technical Paper Series (Inland Waters)*.

Marowski, D. G. (1992). *Environmental Viewpoints*. Gale Group.

Masters, G. M. (2004). *Introduction To Environmental Engineering And Science /2nd Edn*.

Mesner, N., & Geiger, J. (2010). Understanding Your Watershed Fact Sheet: pH. *All Current Publications*, 1252.

Meybeck, M., & Helmer, R. (1989). The quality of rivers: From pristine stage to global pollution. *Palaeogeography, Palaeoclimatology, Palaeoecology*, *75*(4), 283-309.

Michaud, J. P. (1991). *A citizen's guide to understanding and monitoring lakes and streams*. Washington State Department of Ecology, Water Quality Program.

Mohsin, M., Safdar, S., Asghar, F., & Jamal, F. (2013). Assessment of drinking water quality and its impact on residents health in Bahawalpur city. *International Journal of Humanities and Social Science*, *3*, 114-128.

O'Neill, H. J., McKim, K., Chaote, J., & Allen, J. (1994). *Monitoring Surface Water Quality: A Guide for Citizens, Students and Communities in Atlantic Canada*. Environnement Canada.

Perera, A. C., Pelpitiya, I. P., Mowjood, M. I., & Jinadasa, K. B. (2013). Dissolved oxygen dynamics in a stream that flows through a city. A case study in Meda Ela in Kandy. In *Proceeding of the 4th international conference on structural engineering and construction management* (pp. 22-30). Kandy, Sri Lanka.

Pitt, R., Field, R., Lalor, M., & Brown, M. (1995). Urban stormwater toxic pollutants: assessment, sources, and treatability. *Water Environment Research*, *67*(3), 260-275.

Ratnayake, N. (2010). water and environment. *National Forum on Water Research*, 54-69.

Roy, S., Banna, L., Hossain, M., & Rahman, H. (2014). Water quality of Narai canal and Balu river of Dhaka City: An impact of industrialization. *Journal of the Bangladesh Agricultural University*, *12*(2), 285-290.

Senanayake, U. M., Thirumarpan, K., & Thiruchelvam, T. (2016). Water pollution sources, effects and strategies for prevention in Gampaha district. *International Conference on Sustainable Built Environment*, *7*(1).

Settacharnwit, S., Buckney, R. T., & Lim, R. P. (2003). The nutrient status of Nong Han, a shallow tropical lake in north-eastern Thailand: Spatial and temporal variations. *Lakes and Reservoirs: Research and Management*, *8*(3-4), 189-200.

Tevera, D. S., & Moyo, S. (2000). *Environmental Security in Southern Africa*. Sapes Books.

Walker, W. J., McNutt, R. P., & Maslanka, C. K. (1999). The potential contribution of urban runoff to surface sediments of the Passaic River: Sources and chemical characteristics. *Chemosphere, 38*(2), 363-377.

Wijekoon, W., & Herath, G. (2013). Pollution assessment in tributary waters of Mahaweli River around Kandy city. *Proceedings of International Forestry and Environment Symposium, 0*(0).

Wik, A., & Dave, G. (2009). Occurrence and effects of tire wear particles in the environment – A critical review and an initial risk assessment. *Environmental Pollution, 157*(1), 1-11.

Appendix 01

Photographic View of the Study Area

ME1	Inflow from Ampitiya	
ME2	Spillway of Kandy Lake – Point of Origin of Meda Ela	
	Entry Point to the First Open Reach near Sri Lanka Telecom Main Office Kandy	

	First Open Reach Flows through Urbanized Area	
ME3	End of the Underground Section at Deiyannewela	
	Built Up Area Upstream to William Goppallawa Mawatha Bridge	

ME4	Protected with Gabions at Downstream to the Meda Bowala Junction	
	Built up Concrete Drain at Upstream to Heeressagala Junction	
ME5	Meda Ela Confluence	

| MR1 | Upstream of Mahaweli River |  |
| MR1 | Downstream Of Mahaweli River | |